HARDCORE ACCESS

Let's Drive Access to the next level

Richard Thomas
Edwards

CONTENTS

NO LOTS OF TAKING FROM ME

Big introductions are not my style

So, let's cut to the chase. This book isn't about Access Forms, Classes or Modules. There are enough Access writers out there who will show you how to use these things.

Rather, this book is about what you can import, export and attach to and from an Access database and then use what has been exported to produce custom outputs in a variety of outputs which could enhance data visualization.

Originally, I wanted to include ADO, DAO, Odbc, OleDb and SQL Client into the mix but I'm realizing that these Access database related engines deserve their own books as these database related engines also have their own ways of working with Access to accomplish similar tasks and would make this rather straight forward and much less confusing e-book a lot easier to work with.

ACCESS BASICS

It helps to understand the Access Type Library

THE FIRST THING I WANT TO COVER IS THE CREATION OF ACCESS.

There are three ways of doing this directly and an indirect way. The first way is to make a reference to the COM based Access Library and then use the imports statement:

```
Imports Microsoft.Office.Interop
```

Automatically, there are some issues with doing this if you add .Access to the statement above. We have built in functionality in .Net that starts with the word Application. So, using the Microsoft.Office.Interop.Access would immediately cause issues with Application.StartupPath. Anyway, after you have added your imports statement, creating an instance of Access is a one line no brainer:

Dim oAccess As Access.Application = New Access.Application()

Or:

Dim oAccess as Access.Application = CreateObject("Access.Application")

Either way, you now have an instance of Access Running.

The second way is:

Dim oAccess as Object = CreateObject("Access.Application")

The third way is to use Reflection:

```
Dim aType As Type = Type.GetTypeFromProgID("Access.Application")
Dim oAccess As Object = Activator.CreateInstance(aType)
oAccess.Visible = True
```

The Indirect way:

```
Dim ws as object = CreateObject("WScript.Shell")
```

```
Ws.Run("G:\Nwind1.mdb")
```

CREATING DATABASES

Only one at a time

Creating Access Databases is unbelievably easy. All you have to do is create an instance of Access and then use the NewCurrentDatabase function.. Below is an example on how it is done.

```
Const acNewDatabaseFormatUserDefault = &H0 'same as 0
Const acNewDatabaseFormatAccess2000 = &H9 'same as 9
Const acNewDatabaseFormatAccess2002 = &HA 'same as 10
Const acNewDatabaseFormatAccess2007 = &HC 'same as 12


Private Sub Form1_Load(sender As System.Object, e As System.EventArgs) Handles MyBase.Load

Dim oAccess As Object = CreateObject("Access.Application")
oAccess.Visible = True
'Only one at a time here
oAccess.NewCurrentDatabase("G:\MyTest\Access2000\MyA2000.mdb", acNewDatabaseFormatAccess2000)
'oAccess.NewCurrentDatabase("G:\MyTest\Access2002\MyA2002.mdb", acNewDatabaseFormatAccess2002)
'oAccess.NewCurrentDatabase("G:\MyTest\Access2007\MyA2007.accdb", acNewDatabaseFormatAccess2007)
'oAccess.NewCurrentDatabase("G:\MyTest\Access   Default\MyADefault.accdb", acNewDatabaseFormatUserDefault)
```

```
oAccess.Quit()
```

And that is pretty much it. Notice that from 2007 above I used the accdb extension. Access gets picky about that extension and the format used by newer versions of Access.

EXPORTING A TABLE

Let the Games Begin

Personally, I find this to be one of the coolest features Access has to offer to programmers. Take a look at the code below and tell me that isn't going to save you tons of time on creating and populating tables. It took these routine less than 3 seconds to run and it built and filled the Products table from Access 2016 to 2002.

```
Dim aType As Type = Type.GetTypeFromProgID("Access.Application")
Dim oAccess As Object = Activator.CreateInstance(aType)
oAccess.Visible = True

oAccess.DoCmd.TransferDatabase(Microsoft.Office.Interop.Access.Ac
DataTransferType.acExport,
"Microsoft Access",
"G:\MyTest\Access 2002\MyA2002.mdb",
Microsoft.Office.Interop.Access.AcObjectType.acTable, "Products",
"Products", False, False)

oAccess.Quit()
```

Below is an image of the results:

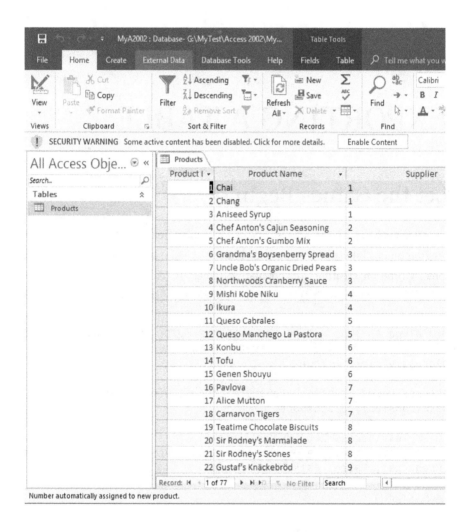

Now, that is totally cool! I could enumerate through all the tables and Views and transfer all of them to my empty databases without having to build all them by hand!

TRANSFERTEXT

This one is a bit harder to do

When I first tried this, the code seemed easy enough to do until I hit the Export Specification. Not anymore. Let's take a look at exporting from an Access Database:

```
Imports Microsoft.Office.Interop
Public Class Form1

Private Sub Form1_Load(sender As System.Object, e As
System.EventArgs) Handles MyBase.Load

Dim oAccess As Access.Application = New Access.Application()

oAccess.OpenCurrentDatabase("G:\Nwind1.accdb")
oAccess.DoCmd.TransferText(Access.AcTextTransferType.acExportDeli
m, , "Products", "G:\mytest\Prodcuts.csv", True, "", 437)

End Sub
End Class
```

Looks simple enough. Simply make a Reference to the Access Library, add the Imports statement above the Public Class Form1 and then copy the code into Form1_Load. Then change the location of the database and the place where you want your CSV file. Run the code and your CSV file is created where you want it.

They all produce exactly the same thing as seen in the image below:

Notice that I didn't include the Access exporter function in these test examples and that while the Format=CSVDelimited was specified the external versions of the exporter function completely bypassed what I specified as the format.

This is a very import point as all the external code did what I wanted it to do.

But when I ran the internal program, Access defaulted to the CSV program until I walked through the wizard and told it I wanted ? as my delimiter and then saved the Products Export Specification shown on the next page.

```
Dim oAccess As Access.Application = New Access.Application()
oAccess.OpenCurrentDatabase("G:\Nwind1.accdb")
oAccess.DoCmd.TransferText(Access.AcTextTransferType.acExportDeli
m, "Products Export Specification", "Products",
"G:\mytest\Prodcuts.txt", True, "", 437)
```

After I deleted the text export file the wizard created and then ran the code above, the text file was generated with ? as the delimiter:

```
"ProductID"?"ProductName"?"SupplierID"?"CategoryID"?"QuantityPerUnit"?"U
1?"Chai"?1?1?"10 boxes x 20 bags"?$18.00?39?0?10?0
2?"Chang"?1?1?"24 - 12 oz bottles"?$19.00?17?40?25?0
3?"Aniseed Syrup"?1?2?"12 - 550 ml bottles"?$10.00?13?70?25?0
```

Well, that's the way the examples showed it.

So, what have we learned so far?

We found out that Access runs the who when it comes down to exporting database tables to text formatted files. That while we can create customized delimited files other than the default csv delimited files, we have to first use the export wizard, create an export specification, delete the text file it creates and then run the Access code with that export specification to get the exporter to work correctly.

EXPORTSPREADSHEET

Where the pedal hits the medal

Access is continuing to amaze me. Now, we've come to one of the largest collections of Export Functions: ExportSpreadsheet. I'm not sure that even I was ready for all of this functionality.

Anyway, here's the code:

```
Dim oAccess As Access.Application = CreateObject("Access.Application")
oAccess.Visible = True
oAccess.OpenCurrentDatabase("G:\Nwind1.accdb")
```

Excel 12

```
oAccess.DoCmd.TransferSpreadsheet(Access.AcDataTransferType.acExport,
Access.AcSpreadSheetType.acSpreadsheetTypeExcel12, "Products",
"c:\Products.xlsx", HasFieldNames:=True)
```

Excel 12XML

```
oAccess.DoCmd.TransferSpreadsheet(Access.AcDataTransferType.acExport,
Access.AcSpreadSheetType.acSpreadsheetTypeExcel12Xml, "Products",
"C:\products.xml", True)
```

Excel 3

```
oAccess.DoCmd.TransferSpreadsheet(Access.AcDataTransferType.acExport,
Access.AcSpreadSheetType.acSpreadsheetTypeExcel3, "Products", "C:\text.xls",
True)
```

Excel 4

```
oAccess.DoCmd.TransferSpreadsheet(Access.AcDataTransferType.acExport,
Access.AcSpreadSheetType.acSpreadsheetTypeExcel4, "Products", "C:\text.xls",
True)
```

Excel 5

```
oAccess.DoCmd.TransferSpreadsheet(Access.AcDataTransferType.acExport,
Access.AcSpreadSheetType.acSpreadsheetTypeExcel5, "Products", "C:\text.xls",
True)
```

Excel 7

```
oAccess.DoCmd.TransferSpreadsheet(Access.AcDataTransferType.acExport,
Access.AcSpreadSheetType.acSpreadsheetTypeExcel7, "Products", "C:\text.xls",
True)
```

Excel 8

```
oAccess.DoCmd.TransferSpreadsheet(Access.AcDataTransferType.acExport,
Access.AcSpreadSheetType.acSpreadsheetTypeExcel8, "Products", "C:\text.xls",
True)
```

Excel 9

```
oAccess.DoCmd.TransferSpreadsheet(Access.AcDataTransferType.acExport,
Access.AcSpreadSheetType.acSpreadsheetTypeExcel9, "Products", "C:\text.xls",
True)
```

Excel 97

```
oAccess.DoCmd.TransferSpreadsheet(Access.AcDataTransferType.acExport,
Access.AcSpreadSheetType.acSpreadsheetTypeExcel97, "Products", "C:\text.xls",
True)
```

Lotus WJ2

```
oAccess.DoCmd.TransferSpreadsheet(Access.AcDataTransferType.acExport,
Access.AcSpreadSheetType.acSpreadsheetTypeLotusWJ2, "Products", "C:\text.wj2",
True)
```

Lotus WK1

```
oAccess.DoCmd.TransferSpreadsheet(Access.AcDataTransferType.acExport,
Access.AcSpreadSheetType.acSpreadsheetTypeLotusWK1, "Products", "C:\text.wk1",
True)
```

Lotus WK3

```
oAccess.DoCmd.TransferSpreadsheet(Access.AcDataTransferType.acExport,
Access.AcSpreadSheetType.acSpreadsheetTypeLotusWK3, "Products", "C:\text.wk3",
True)
```

Lotus WK4

```
oAccess.DoCmd.TransferSpreadsheet(Access.AcDataTransferType.acExport,
Access.AcSpreadSheetType.acSpreadsheetTypeLotusWK4, "Products", "C:\text.wk4",
True)
```

```
oAccess.CloseCurrentDatabase()
oAccess.Quit()
```

Not all of these work despite the fact that the Access 365 says they are available.

EXPORTXML

As good as it gets...Almost

While all of the examples I've created, so far stay within my expectation, the ExportXML doesn't. I is almost as though Microsoft wanted to make things much harder for programmers. Anyway, below is the code.

```
Dim oAccess As Object = Activator.CreateInstance(aType)
oAccess.Visible = True
oAccess.openCurrentDatabase("G:\NWIND1.accdb")
oAccess.ExportXML(ObjectType:=Access.AcExportXMLObjectType.acExportTable,
DataSource:="Products", DataTarget:="C:\Products.xml")
oAccess.CloseCurrentDatabase()
oAcces.Quit()
```

Below is the output:

```xml
-<dataroot generated="2018-07-28T13:40:45">
  -<Products>
      <ProductID>1</ProductID>
      <ProductName>Chai</ProductName>
      <SupplierID>1</SupplierID>
      <CategoryID>1</CategoryID>
      <QuantityPerUnit>10 boxes x 20 bags</QuantityPerUnit>
      <UnitPrice>18</UnitPrice>
      <UnitsInStock>39</UnitsInStock>
      <UnitsOnOrder>0</UnitsOnOrder>
      <ReorderLevel>10</ReorderLevel>
      <Discontinued>0</Discontinued>
  </Products>
  -<Products>
      <ProductID>2</ProductID>
      <ProductName>Chang</ProductName>
      <SupplierID>1</SupplierID>
      <CategoryID>1</CategoryID>
      <QuantityPerUnit>24 - 12 oz bottles</QuantityPerUnit>
      <UnitPrice>19</UnitPrice>
      <UnitsInStock>17</UnitsInStock>
      <UnitsOnOrder>40</UnitsOnOrder>
      <ReorderLevel>25</ReorderLevel>
      <Discontinued>0</Discontinued>
  </Products>
```

CREATING PROGRAMS FOR ACCESS

From ho hum to oh, wow

Let's face it, Access is a great tool for those who live, eat and sleep Access forms, classes and Modules.

But at the end of the day, it is the database, the tables, the views and the queries that allows us to take this Ugly duckling and turn it into a swan.

That is where I enter the picture.

WHAT IS WRONG WITH ACCESS

The rather obvious issue is its inability to have its own database driven system. It still relies on ADO, ADO, DAO, ODBC and OLEDB. In-other-words, Anything beyond the limits of what Access is capable of doing, requires programming skills and that is where we enter the picture.

A COLUMNS OF NAMES, A COLUMN OF VALUES AND COLLECTIONS OF COLUMS KNOWN AS ROWS

A lot of programmers have never heard of Data files commonly known as DAT files. These lightning fast repositories of structured data that gets parsed using a structure or class that uses Get\Set properties as a collection of values.

Below is an example of a structure.

```
Public Structure Student
    <VBFixedString(12)> Public StudentID As String
    <VBFixedString(30)> Public FirstName As String
    <VBFixedString(2)>  Public Mi As String
    <VBFixedString(30)> Public LastName As String
    <VBFixedString(25)> Public Major As String
    <VBFixedString(25)> Public Minor As String
    <VBFixedString(5)>  Public GPA As String
    <VBFixedString(5)>  Public Ranking As String
    <VBFixedString(25)> Public Status As String
End Structure
```

And, of course, the structure is referenced, populated and passed in as a binary write. The opposite happens on the binary read.

Why bother with something like this when delimited or formatted text files perform the same task? Because, WPF DataGridView and Listview , ManagementPacks and SRS Reports must be hard wired with similar kinds of structures or formats to work properly and it has to be done before the program runs making them 100% interactive and programmable.

The structure is actually a row definition table.

ACCESS CODE ESSENTIALS

We have a lot to cover so let's get down to business.

Create An Access Database

```
Public Sub Create_Database(ByVal Filename As String, ByVal Version As String)

    Select Case Version

        Case "2000"

            oAccess = CreateObject("Access.Application")
            oAccess.NewCurrentDataBase(Filename, 9)
            oAccess.Quit()


        Case "2002"

            oAccess = CreateObject("Access.Application")
            oAccess.NewCurrentDataBase(Filename, 10)
            oAccess.Quit()


        Case "2007"
```

```
        oAccess = CreateObject("Access.Application")
        oAccess.NewCurrentDataBase(Filename, 12)
        oAccess.Quit()

    Case "Default"

        oAccess = CreateObject("Access.Application")
        oAccess.NewCurrentDataBase(Filename, 0)
        oAccess.Quit()

    End Select


    End Sub
```

Create An Access Database And Create Table

```
Public Sub Create_Database_And_Create_Table(ByVal Filename As String,
                    ByVal Tablename As String,
                    ByVal fNames() As string,
                    ByVal fTypes() As string,
                    ByVal fSizes() As string,
                    ByVal Version As String)

    Select Case Version

    Case "2000"

        oAccess = CreateObject("Access.Application")
        oAccess.NewCurrentDataBase(Filename, 9)

    Case "2002"

        oAccess = CreateObject("Access.Application")
        oAccess.NewCurrentDataBase(Filename, 10)

    Case "2007"
```

```
            oAccess = CreateObject("Access.Application")
            oAccess.NewCurrentDataBase(Filename, 12)

        Case "Default"

            oAccess = CreateObject("Access.Application")
            oAccess.NewCurrentDataBase(Filename, 0)

    End Select

        Dim db as Object = oAccess.CurrentDb
        Dim tbldef As Object = db.CreateTableDef(Tablename)
        For x as Integer = 0 To fNames.GetLength(0)-1
            Dim fld As Object = Nothing
            If fTypes(x) = "12" then
                fld = tbldef.CreateField(fNames(x), fTypes(x))
            else
                fld = tbldef.CreateField(fNames(x), fTypes(x), fSizes(x))
            End If
            fld.AllowZeroLength = True
            tbldef.Fields.Append(fld)
        Next
        db.TableDefs.Append(tbldef)
        oAccess.CloseCurrentDatabase()
        oAccess.Quit()


    End Sub
```

Create An Access Database, Create and Populate Table

```
 Public Sub Create_Database_Create_Table_And_Populate_Table(ByVal Filename
As String,
                                ByVal Tablename As String,
                                ByVal fNames() As String,
                                ByVal fTypes() As String,
                                ByVal fSizes() As String,
                                ByVal fValues(,) As String,
```

```
                          ByVal Version As String)


Select Case Version

    Case "2000"

        oAccess = CreateObject("Access.Application")
        oAccess.NewCurrentDataBase(Filename, 9)

    Case "2002"

        oAccess = CreateObject("Access.Application")
        oAccess.NewCurrentDataBase(Filename, 10)

    Case "2007"

        oAccess = CreateObject("Access.Application")
        oAccess.NewCurrentDataBase(Filename, 12)

    Case "Default"

        oAccess = CreateObject("Access.Application")
        oAccess.NewCurrentDataBase(Filename, 0)

End Select

        Dim db as Object = oAccess.CurrentDb
        Dim tbldef As Object = db.CreateTableDef(Tablename)
        For x as Integer = 0 To fNames.GetLength(0)-1
            Dim fld As Object = Nothing
            If fTypes(x) = "12" then
                fld = tbldef.CreateField(fNames(x), fTypes(x))
            else
                fld = tbldef.CreateField(fNames(x), fTypes(x), fSizes(x))
            End If
            fld.AllowZeroLength = True
            tbldef.Fields.Append(fld)
        Next
        db.TableDefs.Append(tbldef)
```

```
        Dim rs as Object = db.OpenRecordset(Tablename)

        For y as Integer = 0 To fValues.GetLength(0)-1
          rs.AddNew()
          For x as Integer = 0 To fNames.GetLength(0)-1
            rs.Fields(fNames(x)).Value = fValues(y, x)
          Next
          rs.UpDate()
        Next
        oAccess.CloseCurrentDatabase()
        oAccess.Quit()


    End Sub
```

Create An Access Database, Create and Populate Table, Return Recordset

```
  Public Function CDatabase_CTable_PTable_And_RRecordset(ByVal Filename As
String,
                              ByVal Tablename As String,
                              ByVal fNames() As String,
                              ByVal fTypes() As String,
                              ByVal fSizes() As String,
                              ByVal fValues(,) As String,
                              ByVal Version As String) As Object


    Select Case Version

      Case "2000"

        oAccess = CreateObject("Access.Application")
        oAccess.NewCurrentDataBase(Filename, 9)

      Case "2002"
```

```
    oAccess = CreateObject("Access.Application")
    oAccess.NewCurrentDataBase(Filename, 10)

Case "2007"

    oAccess = CreateObject("Access.Application")
    oAccess.NewCurrentDataBase(Filename, 12)

Case "Default"

    oAccess = CreateObject("Access.Application")
    oAccess.NewCurrentDataBase(Filename, 0)

End Select

    Dim db as Object = oAccess.CurrentDb
    Dim tbldef As Object = db.CreateTableDef(Tablename)
    For x as Integer = 0 To fNames.GetLength(0)-1
       Dim fld As Object = Nothing
       If fTypes(x) = "12" then
          fld = tbldef.CreateField(fNames(x), fTypes(x))
       else
          fld = tbldef.CreateField(fNames(x), fTypes(x), fSizes(x))
       End If
       fld.AllowZeroLength = True
       tbldef.Fields.Append(fld)
    Next
    db.TableDefs.Append(tbldef)

    Dim rs as Object = db.OpenRecordset(Tablename)

    For y as Integer = 0 To fValues.GetLength(0)-1
       rs.AddNew()
       For x as Integer = 0 To fNames.GetLength(0)-1
          rs.Fields(fNames(x)).Value = fValues(y, x)
       Next
       rs.UpDate()
    Next
    return rs
    oAccess.CloseCurrentDatabase()
```

```
        oAccess.Quit()


End Sub
```

Open Access Database and Create Table

```
Public Sub OpenDatabase_CTable(ByVal Filename As String,
                ByVal Tablename As String,
                ByVal fNames() As String,
                ByVal fTypes() As String,
                ByVal fSizes() As String)



   Dim oAccess As Object = CreateObject("Access.Application")
   oAccess.OpenCurrentDataBase(Filename)

   Dim db as Object = oAccess.CurrentDb
   Dim tbldef As Object = db.CreateTableDef(Tablename)
   For x as Integer = 0 To fNames.GetLength(0)-1
      Dim fld As Object = Nothing
      If fTypes(x) = "12" then
         fld = tbldef.CreateField(fNames(x), fTypes(x))
      else
         fld = tbldef.CreateField(fNames(x), fTypes(x), fSizes(x))
      End If
      fld.AllowZeroLength = True
      tbldef.Fields.Append(fld)
   Next
   db.TableDefs.Append(tbldef)
   oAccess.CloseCurrentDatabase()
   oAccess.Quit()


End Sub
```

Open Access Database, Create and Populate Table, Return Recordset

```
Public Function OpenDatabase_CTable_PTable_Return_Recordset(ByVal Filename
As String,
                              ByVal Tablename As String,
                              ByVal fNames() As String,
                              ByVal fTypes() As String,
                              ByVal fSizes() As String,
                              ByVal fValues(,) As String) As Object


   Dim oAccess As Object = CreateObject("Access.Application")
   oAccess.OpenCurrentDataBase(Filename)

   Dim db as Object = oAccess.CurrentDb
   Dim tbldef As Object = db.CreateTableDef(Tablename)
   For x as Integer = 0 To fNames.GetLength(0)-1
      Dim fld As Object = Nothing
      If fTypes(x) = "12" then
         fld = tbldef.CreateField(fNames(x), fTypes(x))
      else
         fld = tbldef.CreateField(fNames(x), fTypes(x), fSizes(x))
      End If
      fld.AllowZeroLength = True
      tbldef.Fields.Append(fld)
   Next
   db.TableDefs.Append(tbldef)

   Dim rs as Object = db.OpenRecordset(Tablename)

   For y as Integer = 0 To fValues.GetLength(0)-1
      rs.AddNew()
      For x as Integer = 0 To fNames.GetLength(0)-1
         rs.Fields(fNames(x)).Value = fValues(y, x)
      Next
      rs.UpDate()
   Next
```

```
    return rs
oAccess.CloseCurrentDatabase()
oAccess.Quit()

  End Sub
```

Open Access Database and Populate Table

```
Public Sub OpenDatabase_PTable(ByVal Filename As String,
            ByVal Tablename As String,
            ByVal fValues(,) As String)


Dim oAccess As Object = CreateObject("Access.Application")
oAccess.OpenCurrentDataBase(Filename)

Dim db as Object = oAccess.CurrentDb

Dim rs as Object = db.OpenRecordset(Tablename)
For y as Integer = 0 To fValues.GetLength(0)-1
  rs.AddNew()
  For x as Integer = 0 To fNames.GetLength(0)-1
    rs.Fields(fNames(x)).Value = fValues(y, x)
  Next
  rs.UpDate()
Next
oAccess.CloseCurrentDatabase()
oAccess.Quit()

  End Sub
```

Open Access Database, Populate Table and Return Recordset

```
Public  Function  OpenDatabase_PTable_Return_Recordset(ByVal  Filename  As
String,
            ByVal Tablename As String,
            ByVal fValues(,) As String) As Object
```

```
Dim oAccess As Object = CreateObject("Access.Application")
oAccess.OpenCurrentDataBase(Filename)

Dim db as Object = oAccess.CurrentDb

Dim rs as Object = db.OpenRecordset(Tablename)
For y as Integer = 0 To fValues.GetLength(0)-1
  rs.AddNew()
  For x as Integer = 0 To fNames.GetLength(0)-1
    rs.Fields(fNames(x)).Value = fValues(y, x)
  Next
  rs.UpDate()
Next
Return rs
oAccess.CloseCurrentDatabase()
oAccess.Quit()

End Function
```

Open Access Database and Return Recordset

```
Public Function OpenDatabase_Return_Recordset(ByVal Filename As String,
          ByVal Tablename As String) As Object

  Dim oAccess As Object = CreateObject("Access.Application")
  oAccess.OpenCurrentDataBase(Filename)

  Dim db as Object = oAccess.CurrentDb
  Dim rs as Object = db.OpenRecordset(Tablename)

  return rs

  oAccess.CloseCurrentDatabase()
  oAccess.Quit()
```

End Function

Now, that was fun! Okay, we now have initialization code for creating and opening Access databases, creating and populating tables and returning recordsets.

But just because we used Access to help us with a handle to a database that Access manages does mean Access should always get the credit for the rest of the heavy lifting. In fact, isn't that DAO that is used to create the TableDefs, Dao that helps to build the table and DAO that populates and returns the recordset?

STOCK DAO INITIALIZTION ROUTINES

Nothing like the smell of DAO in the Morning

And Off we go!

Below are the various DAO "supposedly" supports:

dbVersion10
dbVersion11
dbVersion20
dbVersion30
dbVersion40
dbVersion120
dbVersion140
dbVersion150
dbVersion167

I say supposedly because the last time I looked DAO.DBEngine.36 supported up to dbVersion40.

Create Database

```
Public Sub Create_Database(ByVal Filename As String, ByVal Version As String)
```

```vbnet
Dim DBEngine as Object = CreateObject("DAO.DBEngine.36")
Dim db as Object = Nothing


Select Case Version

        Case "1"

        db = DBEngine.CreateDatabase("C:\version1.mdb",
Dao.LanguageConstants.dbLangGeneral,
Dao.DatabaseTypeEnum.dbVersion10)

        Case "11"

        db = DBEngine.CreateDatabase("C:\version11.mdb",
Dao.LanguageConstants.dbLangGeneral,
Dao.DatabaseTypeEnum.dbVersion11)

        Case "2"

        db = DBEngine.CreateDatabase("C:\version2.mdb",
Dao.LanguageConstants.dbLangGeneral,
Dao.DatabaseTypeEnum.dbVersion20)

        Case "3"

        db = DBEngine.CreateDatabase("C:\version3.mdb",
Dao.LanguageConstants.dbLangGeneral,
Dao.DatabaseTypeEnum.dbVersion30)

        Case "4"

        db = DBEngine.CreateDatabase("C:\version4.mdb",
Dao.LanguageConstants.dbLangGeneral,
Dao.DatabaseTypeEnum.dbVersion40)

        Case "120"

        db = DBEngine.CreateDatabase("C:\Version120.mdb",
Dao.LanguageConstants.dbLangGeneral,
Dao.DatabaseTypeEnum.dbVersion120)

        Case "140"
```

```
        db = DBEngine.CreateDatabase("C:\Version140.mdb",
Dao.LanguageConstants.dbLangGeneral,
Dao.DatabaseTypeEnum.dbVersion140)


        Case "150"


        db = DBEngine.CreateDatabase("C:\Version150.mdb",
Dao.LanguageConstants.dbLangGeneral,
Dao.DatabaseTypeEnum.dbVersion150)
```

End Select

End Sub

Create Database And Create Table

Public Sub Create_Database_And_Create_Table(ByVal Filename As String,
                        ByVal Tablename As String,
                        ByVal fNames() As string,
                        ByVal fTypes() As string,
                        ByVal fSizes() As string,
                        ByVal Version As String)

        Dim DBEngine as Object = CreateObject("DAO.DBEngine.36")
        Dim db as Object = Nothing

        Select Case Version

```
        Case "1"

        db = DBEngine.CreateDatabase("C:\version1.mdb",
Dao.LanguageConstants.dbLangGeneral,
Dao.DatabaseTypeEnum.dbVersion10)
```

```
        Case "11"

            db = DBEngine.CreateDatabase("C:\version11.mdb",
Dao.LanguageConstants.dbLangGeneral,
Dao.DatabaseTypeEnum.dbVersion11)

        Case "2"

            db = DBEngine.CreateDatabase("C:\version2.mdb",
Dao.LanguageConstants.dbLangGeneral,
Dao.DatabaseTypeEnum.dbVersion20)

        Case "3"

            db = DBEngine.CreateDatabase("C:\version3.mdb",
Dao.LanguageConstants.dbLangGeneral,
Dao.DatabaseTypeEnum.dbVersion30)

        Case "4"

            db = DBEngine.CreateDatabase("C:\version4.mdb",
Dao.LanguageConstants.dbLangGeneral,
Dao.DatabaseTypeEnum.dbVersion40)

        Case "120"

            db = DBEngine.CreateDatabase("C:\Version120.mdb",
Dao.LanguageConstants.dbLangGeneral,
Dao.DatabaseTypeEnum.dbVersion120)

        Case "140"

            db = DBEngine.CreateDatabase("C:\Version140.mdb",
Dao.LanguageConstants.dbLangGeneral,
Dao.DatabaseTypeEnum.dbVersion140)

        Case "150"


            db = DBEngine.CreateDatabase("C:\Version150.mdb",
Dao.LanguageConstants.dbLangGeneral,
Dao.DatabaseTypeEnum.dbVersion150)

    End Select
```

```
Dim tbldef As Object = db.CreateTableDef(Tablename)
For x as Integer = 0 To fNames.GetLength(0)-1
   Dim fld As Object = Nothing
   If fTypes(x) = "12" then
      fld = tbldef.CreateField(fNames(x), fTypes(x))
   else
      fld = tbldef.CreateField(fNames(x), fTypes(x), fSizes(x))
   End If
   fld.AllowZeroLength = True
   tbldef.Fields.Append(fld)
Next
db.TableDefs.Append(tbldef)

End Sub
```

Create Database, Create and Populate Table

```
Public Sub Create_Database_Create_Table_And_Populate_Table(ByVal Filename
As String,
                        ByVal Tablename As String,
                        ByVal fNames() As String,
                        ByVal fTypes() As String,
                        ByVal fSizes() As String,
                        ByVal fValues(,) As String,
                        ByVal Version As String)

Dim DBEngine as Object = CreateObject("DAO.DBEngine.36")
Dim db as Object = Nothing


Select Case Version

     Case "1"

     db = DBEngine.CreateDatabase("C:\version1.mdb",
Dao.LanguageConstants.dbLangGeneral,
Dao.DatabaseTypeEnum.dbVersion10)
```

```
Case "11"

    db = DBEngine.CreateDatabase("C:\version11.mdb",
Dao.LanguageConstants.dbLangGeneral,
Dao.DatabaseTypeEnum.dbVersion11)

    Case "2"

    db = DBEngine.CreateDatabase("C:\version2.mdb",
Dao.LanguageConstants.dbLangGeneral,
Dao.DatabaseTypeEnum.dbVersion20)

    Case "3"

    db = DBEngine.CreateDatabase("C:\version3.mdb",
Dao.LanguageConstants.dbLangGeneral,
Dao.DatabaseTypeEnum.dbVersion30)

    Case "4"

    db = DBEngine.CreateDatabase("C:\version4.mdb",
Dao.LanguageConstants.dbLangGeneral,
Dao.DatabaseTypeEnum.dbVersion40)

    Case "120"

    db = DBEngine.CreateDatabase("C:\Version120.mdb",
Dao.LanguageConstants.dbLangGeneral,
Dao.DatabaseTypeEnum.dbVersion120)

    Case "140"

    db = DBEngine.CreateDatabase("C:\Version140.mdb",
Dao.LanguageConstants.dbLangGeneral,
Dao.DatabaseTypeEnum.dbVersion140)


    Case "150"


    db = DBEngine.CreateDatabase("C:\Version150.mdb",
Dao.LanguageConstants.dbLangGeneral,
Dao.DatabaseTypeEnum.dbVersion150)
```

```
      End Select

          Dim tbldef As Object = db.CreateTableDef(Tablename)
          For x as Integer = 0 To fNames.GetLength(0)-1
            Dim fld As Object = Nothing
            If fTypes(x) = "12" then
               fld = tbldef.CreateField(fNames(x), fTypes(x))
            else
               fld = tbldef.CreateField(fNames(x), fTypes(x), fSizes(x))
            End If
            fld.AllowZeroLength = True
            tbldef.Fields.Append(fld)
          Next
          db.TableDefs.Append(tbldef)

          Dim rs as Object = db.OpenRecordset(Tablename)

          For y as Integer = 0 To fValues.GetLength(0)-1
            rs.AddNew()
            For x as Integer = 0 To fNames.GetLength(0)-1
               rs.Fields(fNames(x)).Value = fValues(y, x)
            Next
            rs.UpDate()
          Next

      End Sub
```

Create Database, Create and Populate Table, Return Recordset

```
   Public Function CDatabase_CTable_PTable_And_RRecordset(ByVal Filename As
String,
                         ByVal Tablename As String,
                         ByVal fNames() As String,
                         ByVal fTypes() As String,
                         ByVal fSizes() As String,
                         ByVal fValues(,) As String,
                         ByVal Version As String) As Object
```

```
Dim DBEngine as Object = CreateObject("DAO.DBEngine.36")
Dim db as Object = Nothing

Select Case Version

        Case "1"

        db = DBEngine.CreateDatabase("C:\version1.mdb",
Dao.LanguageConstants.dbLangGeneral,
Dao.DatabaseTypeEnum.dbVersion10)

        Case "11"

        db = DBEngine.CreateDatabase("C:\version11.mdb",
Dao.LanguageConstants.dbLangGeneral,
Dao.DatabaseTypeEnum.dbVersion11)

        Case "2"

        db = DBEngine.CreateDatabase("C:\version2.mdb",
Dao.LanguageConstants.dbLangGeneral,
Dao.DatabaseTypeEnum.dbVersion20)

        Case "3"

        db = DBEngine.CreateDatabase("C:\version3.mdb",
Dao.LanguageConstants.dbLangGeneral,
Dao.DatabaseTypeEnum.dbVersion30)

        Case "4"

        db = DBEngine.CreateDatabase("C:\version4.mdb",
Dao.LanguageConstants.dbLangGeneral,
Dao.DatabaseTypeEnum.dbVersion40)

        Case "120"

        db = DBEngine.CreateDatabase("C:\Version120.mdb",
Dao.LanguageConstants.dbLangGeneral,
Dao.DatabaseTypeEnum.dbVersion120)

        Case "140"
```

```
        db = DBEngine.CreateDatabase("C:\Version140.mdb",
Dao.LanguageConstants.dbLangGeneral,
Dao.DatabaseTypeEnum.dbVersion140)


        Case "150"

        db = DBEngine.CreateDatabase("C:\Version150.mdb",
Dao.LanguageConstants.dbLangGeneral,
Dao.DatabaseTypeEnum.dbVersion150)


    End Select

        Dim tbldef As Object = db.CreateTableDef(Tablename)
        For x as Integer = 0 To fNames.GetLength(0)-1
          Dim fld As Object = Nothing
          If fTypes(x) = "12" then
            fld = tbldef.CreateField(fNames(x), fTypes(x))
          else
            fld = tbldef.CreateField(fNames(x), fTypes(x), fSizes(x))
          End If
          fld.AllowZeroLength = True
          tbldef.Fields.Append(fld)
        Next
        db.TableDefs.Append(tbldef)

        Dim rs as Object = db.OpenRecordset(Tablename)

        For y as Integer = 0 To fValues.GetLength(0)-1
          rs.AddNew()
          For x as Integer = 0 To fNames.GetLength(0)-1
            rs.Fields(fNames(x)).Value = fValues(y, x)
          Next
          rs.UpDate()
        Next
        return rs

    End Sub
```

Open Database and Create Table

```
Public Sub OpenDatabase_CTable(ByVal Filename As String,
                ByVal Tablename As String,
                ByVal fNames() As String,
                ByVal fTypes() As String,
                ByVal fSizes() As String)



    Dim DBEngine as Object = CreateObject("DAO.DBEngine.36")
    Dim db as Object =DBEngine.OpenDatabase(Filename)

    Dim db as Object = oAccess.CurrentDb
    Dim tbldef As Object = db.CreateTableDef(Tablename)
    For x as Integer = 0 To fNames.GetLength(0)-1
        Dim fld As Object = Nothing
        If fTypes(x) = "12" then
            fld = tbldef.CreateField(fNames(x), fTypes(x))
        else
            fld = tbldef.CreateField(fNames(x), fTypes(x), fSizes(x))
        End If
        fld.AllowZeroLength = True
        tbldef.Fields.Append(fld)
    Next
    db.TableDefs.Append(tbldef)

End Sub
```

Open Database, Create and Populate Table, Return Recordset

```
Public Function OpenDatabase_CTable_PTable_Return_Recordset(ByVal Filename
As String,
                    ByVal Tablename As String,
                    ByVal fNames() As String,
                    ByVal fTypes() As String,
```

```
                    ByVal fSizes() As String,
                    ByVal fValues(,) As String) As Object


      Dim DBEngine as Object = CreateObject("DAO.DBEngine.36")
      Dim db as Object =DBEngine.OpenDatabase(Filename)

      Dim tbldef As Object = db.CreateTableDef(Tablename)
      For x as Integer = 0 To fNames.GetLength(0)-1
         Dim fld As Object = Nothing
         If fTypes(x) = "12" then
            fld = tbldef.CreateField(fNames(x), fTypes(x))
         else
            fld = tbldef.CreateField(fNames(x), fTypes(x), fSizes(x))
         End If
         fld.AllowZeroLength = True
         tbldef.Fields.Append(fld)
      Next
      db.TableDefs.Append(tbldef)

      Dim rs as Object = db.OpenRecordset(Tablename)

      For y as Integer = 0 To fValues.GetLength(0)-1
         rs.AddNew()
         For x as Integer = 0 To fNames.GetLength(0)-1
            rs.Fields(fNames(x)).Value = fValues(y, x)
         Next
         rs.UpDate()
      Next
      return rs
   End Sub
```

Open Database and Populate Table

```
   Public Sub OpenDatabase_PTable(ByVal Filename As String,
                    ByVal Tablename As String,
                    ByVal fValues(,) As String)
```

```
Dim DBEngine as Object = CreateObject("DAO.DBEngine.36")
Dim db as Object =DBEngine.OpenDatabase(Filename)

Dim rs as Object = db.OpenRecordset(Tablename)
For y as Integer = 0 To fValues.GetLength(0)-1
  rs.AddNew()
  For x as Integer = 0 To fNames.GetLength(0)-1
    rs.Fields(fNames(x)).Value = fValues(y, x)
  Next
  rs.UpDate()
Next

End Sub
```

Open Database, Populate Table and Return Recordset

```
Public  Function  OpenDatabase_PTable_Return_Recordset(ByVal  Filename  As
String,
                ByVal Tablename As String,
                ByVal fValues(,) As String) As Object

Dim DBEngine as Object = CreateObject("DAO.DBEngine.36")
Dim db as Object =DBEngine.OpenDatabase(Filename)

Dim rs as Object = db.OpenRecordset(Tablename)
For y as Integer = 0 To fValues.GetLength(0)-1
  rs.AddNew()
  For x as Integer = 0 To fNames.GetLength(0)-1
    rs.Fields(fNames(x)).Value = fValues(y, x)
  Next
  rs.UpDate()
Next

return rs

End Function
```

Open Database and Return Recordset

```
Public Function OpenDatabase_Return_Recordset(ByVal Filename As String,
               ByVal Tablename As String) As Object


   Dim DBEngine as Object = CreateObject("DAO.DBEngine.36")
   Dim db as Object =DBEngine.OpenDatabase(Filename)

   Dim rs as Object = db.OpenRecordset(Tablename)

   return rs

End Function
```

USING THE DAO
WORKSPACE AND ODBC

Yes, you can use ODBC but not to create the databases.

We're going to be using the same patterns as we did with the DAO routines above.

Create Database

Public Sub Create_Database(ByVal Filename As String, ByVal Version As String)

```
Dim DBEngine As Dao.DBEngine = CreateObject("DAO.DBEngine.36")
Dim wspace As Dao.Workspace = DBEngine.Workspaces(0)
Dim db As Dao.Database = Nothing

Select Case Version

    Case "1"

        db = wspace.CreateDatabase("C:\Version1.mdb",
Dao.LanguageConstants.dbLangGeneral,
Dao.DatabaseTypeEnum.dbVersion10)

    Case "11"
```

```vb
        db = wspace.CreateDatabase("C:\Version11.mdb",
Dao.LanguageConstants.dbLangGeneral,
Dao.DatabaseTypeEnum.dbVersion11)


    Case "2"


        db = wspace.CreateDatabase("C:\Version2.mdb",
Dao.LanguageConstants.dbLangGeneral,
Dao.DatabaseTypeEnum.dbVersion20)


    Case "3"


        db = wspace.CreateDatabase("C:\Version3.mdb",
Dao.LanguageConstants.dbLangGeneral,
Dao.DatabaseTypeEnum.dbVersion30)


    Case "120"


        db = wspace.CreateDatabase("C:\Version120.accdb",
Dao.LanguageConstants.dbLangGeneral,
Dao.DatabaseTypeEnum.dbVersion120)

    Case "140"

        db = wspace.CreateDatabase("C:\Version140.accdb",
Dao.LanguageConstants.dbLangGeneral,
Dao.DatabaseTypeEnum.dbVersion140)

    Case "150"

        db = wspace.CreateDatabase("C:\Version150.accdb",
Dao.LanguageConstants.dbLangGeneral,
Dao.DatabaseTypeEnum.dbVersion150)

End Select

End Sub
```

Create Database And Create Table

```
Public Sub Create_Database_And_Create_Table(ByVal Filename As String,
                        ByVal Tablename As String,
                        ByVal fNames() As string,
                        ByVal fTypes() As string,
                        ByVal fSizes() As string,
                        ByVal Version As String)



Dim DBEngine As Dao.DBEngine = CreateObject("DAO.DBEngine.36")
Dim wspace As Dao.Workspace = DBEngine.Workspaces(0)
Dim db As Dao.Database = Nothing

Select Case Version

    Case "1"

        db = wspace.CreateDatabase("C:\Version1.mdb",
Dao.LanguageConstants.dbLangGeneral,
Dao.DatabaseTypeEnum.dbVersion10)

    Case "11"



        db = wspace.CreateDatabase("C:\Version11.mdb",
Dao.LanguageConstants.dbLangGeneral,
Dao.DatabaseTypeEnum.dbVersion11)


    Case "2"


        db = wspace.CreateDatabase("C:\Version2.mdb",
Dao.LanguageConstants.dbLangGeneral,
Dao.DatabaseTypeEnum.dbVersion20)


    Case "3"
```

```
        db = wspace.CreateDatabase("C:\Version3.mdb",
Dao.LanguageConstants.dbLangGeneral,
Dao.DatabaseTypeEnum.dbVersion30)


    Case "120"


        db = wspace.CreateDatabase("C:\Version120.accdb",
Dao.LanguageConstants.dbLangGeneral,
Dao.DatabaseTypeEnum.dbVersion120)

    Case "140"

        db = wspace.CreateDatabase("C:\Version140.accdb",
Dao.LanguageConstants.dbLangGeneral,
Dao.DatabaseTypeEnum.dbVersion140)

    Case "150"

        db = wspace.CreateDatabase("C:\Version150.accdb",
Dao.LanguageConstants.dbLangGeneral,
Dao.DatabaseTypeEnum.dbVersion150)

End Select

        Dim tbldef As Object = db.CreateTableDef(Tablename)
        For x as Integer = 0 To fNames.GetLength(0)-1
          Dim fld As Object = Nothing
          If fTypes(x) = "12" then
            fld = tbldef.CreateField(fNames(x), fTypes(x))
          else
            fld = tbldef.CreateField(fNames(x), fTypes(x), fSizes(x))
          End If
          fld.AllowZeroLength = True
          tbldef.Fields.Append(fld)
        Next
        db.TableDefs.Append(tbldef)


    End Sub
```

Create Database, Create and Populate Table

Public Sub Create_Database_Create_Table_And_Populate_Table(ByVal Filename As String,

> ByVal Tablename As String,
> ByVal fNames() As String,
> ByVal fTypes() As String,
> ByVal fSizes() As String,
> ByVal fValues(,) As String,
> ByVal Version As String)

```
    Dim DBEngine as Object = CreateObject("DAO.DBEngine.36")
    Dim db as Object = Nothing

Select Case Version

    Case "1"

        db = wspace.CreateDatabase("C:\Version1.mdb",
Dao.LanguageConstants.dbLangGeneral,
Dao.DatabaseTypeEnum.dbVersion10)

    Case "11"



        db = wspace.CreateDatabase("C:\Version11.mdb",
Dao.LanguageConstants.dbLangGeneral,
Dao.DatabaseTypeEnum.dbVersion11)


    Case "2"


        db = wspace.CreateDatabase("C:\Version2.mdb",
Dao.LanguageConstants.dbLangGeneral,
Dao.DatabaseTypeEnum.dbVersion20)


    Case "3"
```

```vb
        db = wspace.CreateDatabase("C:\Version3.mdb",
Dao.LanguageConstants.dbLangGeneral,
Dao.DatabaseTypeEnum.dbVersion30)


    Case "120"


        db = wspace.CreateDatabase("C:\Version120.accdb",
Dao.LanguageConstants.dbLangGeneral,
Dao.DatabaseTypeEnum.dbVersion120)

    Case "140"

        db = wspace.CreateDatabase("C:\Version140.accdb",
Dao.LanguageConstants.dbLangGeneral,
Dao.DatabaseTypeEnum.dbVersion140)

    Case "150"

        db = wspace.CreateDatabase("C:\Version150.accdb",
Dao.LanguageConstants.dbLangGeneral,
Dao.DatabaseTypeEnum.dbVersion150)

End Select

        Dim tbldef As Object = db.CreateTableDef(Tablename)
        For x as Integer = 0 To fNames.GetLength(0)-1
            Dim fld As Object = Nothing
            If fTypes(x) = "12" then
                fld = tbldef.CreateField(fNames(x), fTypes(x))
            else
                fld = tbldef.CreateField(fNames(x), fTypes(x), fSizes(x))
            End If
            fld.AllowZeroLength = True
            tbldef.Fields.Append(fld)
        Next
        db.TableDefs.Append(tbldef)

        Dim rs as Object = db.OpenRecordset(Tablename)
```

```
        For y as Integer = 0 To fValues.GetLength(0)-1
          rs.AddNew()
          For x as Integer = 0 To fNames.GetLength(0)-1
            rs.Fields(fNames(x)).Value = fValues(y, x)
          Next
          rs.UpDate()
        Next

    End Sub
```

Create Database, Create and Populate Table, Return Recordset

```
    Public Function CDatabase_CTable_PTable_And_RRecordset(ByVal Filename As
String,
                        ByVal Tablename As String,
                        ByVal fNames() As String,
                        ByVal fTypes() As String,
                        ByVal fSizes() As String,
                        ByVal fValues(,) As String,
                        ByVal Version As String) As Object


      Dim DBEngine as Object = CreateObject("DAO.DBEngine.36")

      Dim db as Object = Nothing

Select Case Version

    Case "1"

        db = wspace.CreateDatabase("C:\Version1.mdb",
Dao.LanguageConstants.dbLangGeneral,
Dao.DatabaseTypeEnum.dbVersion10)

    Case "11"
```

```vb
        db = wspace.CreateDatabase("C:\Version11.mdb",
Dao.LanguageConstants.dbLangGeneral,
Dao.DatabaseTypeEnum.dbVersion11)


    Case "2"


        db = wspace.CreateDatabase("C:\Version2.mdb",
Dao.LanguageConstants.dbLangGeneral,
Dao.DatabaseTypeEnum.dbVersion20)


    Case "3"


        db = wspace.CreateDatabase("C:\Version3.mdb",
Dao.LanguageConstants.dbLangGeneral,
Dao.DatabaseTypeEnum.dbVersion30)


    Case "120"


        db = wspace.CreateDatabase("C:\Version120.accdb",
Dao.LanguageConstants.dbLangGeneral,
Dao.DatabaseTypeEnum.dbVersion120)

    Case "140"

        db = wspace.CreateDatabase("C:\Version140.accdb",
Dao.LanguageConstants.dbLangGeneral,
Dao.DatabaseTypeEnum.dbVersion140)

    Case "150"

        db = wspace.CreateDatabase("C:\Version150.accdb",
Dao.LanguageConstants.dbLangGeneral,
Dao.DatabaseTypeEnum.dbVersion150)

End Select

        Dim tbldef As Object = db.CreateTableDef(Tablename)
        For x as Integer = 0 To fNames.GetLength(0)-1
```

```
            Dim fld As Object = Nothing
            If fTypes(x) = "12" then
               fld = tbldef.CreateField(fNames(x), fTypes(x))
            else
               fld = tbldef.CreateField(fNames(x), fTypes(x), fSizes(x))
            End If
            fld.AllowZeroLength = True
            tbldef.Fields.Append(fld)
         Next
         db.TableDefs.Append(tbldef)

         Dim rs as Object = db.OpenRecordset(Tablename)

         For y as Integer = 0 To fValues.GetLength(0)-1
            rs.AddNew()
            For x as Integer = 0 To fNames.GetLength(0)-1
               rs.Fields(fNames(x)).Value = fValues(y, x)
            Next
            rs.UpDate()
         Next

         return rs

   End Function
```

Open Database and Create Table

```
   Public Sub OpenDatabase_CTable(ByVal Filename As String,
                     ByVal Tablename As String,
                     ByVal fNames() As String,
                     ByVal fTypes() As String,
                     ByVal fSizes() As String)



      Dim ws As Dao.Workspace =
   DBEngine.CreateWorkspace("ODBCWorkSpace", "", "",
   Dao.WorkspaceTypeEnum.dbUseODBC)
```

```vbnet
    Dim db As Dao.Database = ws.OpenDatabase("", False, False,
"ODBC;Driver={Microsoft Access Driver (*.mdb)};dbq=C:\" &
filename)

    Dim tbldef As Object = db.CreateTableDef(Tablename)
    For x as Integer = 0 To fNames.GetLength(0)-1
        Dim fld As Object = Nothing
        If fTypes(x) = "12" then
            fld = tbldef.CreateField(fNames(x), fTypes(x))
        else
            fld = tbldef.CreateField(fNames(x), fTypes(x), fSizes(x))
        End If
        fld.AllowZeroLength = True
        tbldef.Fields.Append(fld)
    Next
    db.TableDefs.Append(tbldef)

End Sub
```

Open Database, Create and Populate Table, Return Recordset

```vbnet
    Public Function OpenDatabase_CTable_PTable_Return_Recordset(ByVal Filename
As String,
                            ByVal Tablename As String,
                            ByVal fNames() As String,
                            ByVal fTypes() As String,
                            ByVal fSizes() As String,
                            ByVal fValues(,) As String) As Object


    Dim ws As Dao.Workspace =
DBEngine.CreateWorkspace("ODBCWorkSpace", "", "",
Dao.WorkspaceTypeEnum.dbUseODBC)
    Dim db As Dao.Database = ws.OpenDatabase("", False, False,
"ODBC;Driver={Microsoft Access Driver (*.mdb)};dbq=C:\" &
filename)
```

```vb
        Dim tbldef As Object = db.CreateTableDef(Tablename)
        For x as Integer = 0 To fNames.GetLength(0)-1
            Dim fld As Object = Nothing
            If fTypes(x) = "12" then
                fld = tbldef.CreateField(fNames(x), fTypes(x))
            else
                fld = tbldef.CreateField(fNames(x), fTypes(x), fSizes(x))
            End If
            fld.AllowZeroLength = True
            tbldef.Fields.Append(fld)
        Next
        db.TableDefs.Append(tbldef)

        Dim rs as Object = db.OpenRecordset(Tablename)

        For y as Integer = 0 To fValues.GetLength(0)-1
            rs.AddNew()
            For x as Integer = 0 To fNames.GetLength(0)-1
                rs.Fields(fNames(x)).Value = fValues(y, x)
            Next
            rs.UpDate()
        Next
        return rs
    End Sub
```

Open Database and Populate Table

```vb
    Public Sub OpenDatabase_PTable(ByVal Filename As String,
                    ByVal Tablename As String,
                    ByVal fValues(,) As String)


    Dim ws As Dao.Workspace =
DBEngine.CreateWorkspace("ODBCWorkSpace", "", "",
Dao.WorkspaceTypeEnum.dbUseODBC)
    Dim db As Dao.Database = ws.OpenDatabase("", False, False,
"ODBC;Driver={Microsoft Access Driver (*.mdb)};dbq=C:\" &
filename)
```

```
   Dim rs as Object = db.OpenRecordset(Tablename)
   For y as Integer = 0 To fValues.GetLength(0)-1
     rs.AddNew()
     For x as Integer = 0 To fNames.GetLength(0)-1
       rs.Fields(fNames(x)).Value = fValues(y, x)
     Next
     rs.UpDate()
   Next

 End Sub
```

Open Database, Populate Table and Return Recordset

```
   Public   Function   OpenDatabase_PTable_Return_Recordset(ByVal   Filename   As
String,
               ByVal Tablename As String,
               ByVal fValues(,) As String) As Object


   Dim ws As Dao.Workspace =
DBEngine.CreateWorkspace("ODBCWorkSpace", "", "",
Dao.WorkspaceTypeEnum.dbUseODBC)
   Dim db As Dao.Database = ws.OpenDatabase("", False, False,
"ODBC;Driver={Microsoft Access Driver (*.mdb)};dbq=C:\" &
filename)

   Dim rs as Object = db.OpenRecordset(Tablename)
   For y as Integer = 0 To fValues.GetLength(0)-1
     rs.AddNew()
     For x as Integer = 0 To fNames.GetLength(0)-1
       rs.Fields(fNames(x)).Value = fValues(y, x)
     Next
     rs.UpDate()
   Next

   return rs

 End Function
```

Open Database and Return Recordset

Public Function OpenDatabase_Return_Recordset(ByVal Filename As String, ByVal Tablename As String) As Object

```
    Dim ws As Dao.Workspace =
DBEngine.CreateWorkspace("ODBCWorkSpace", "", "",
Dao.WorkspaceTypeEnum.dbUseODBC)
    Dim db As Dao.Database = ws.OpenDatabase("", False, False,
"ODBC;Driver={Microsoft Access Driver (*.mdb)};dbq=C:\" &
filename)
```

Dim rs as Object = db.OpenRecordset(Tablename)

return rs

End Function

ADOX AND DAO DATABASES

ADOX has the ability to create databases. It uses the Jet

Create Database

Public Sub Create_Database(ByVal Filename As String, ByVal Version As String)

```
    Dim ocat As Object = CreateObject("ADOX.Catalog")

    Select Case Version

       Case "1"

              ocat.Create("Provider=Microsoft.Jet.OLEDB.4.0;Jet
OLEDB:Engine Type=1;Data Source=" & Filename)


       Case "11"

              ocat.Create("Provider=Microsoft.Jet.OLEDB.4.0;Jet
OLEDB:Engine Type=2;Data Source=" & Filename)


       Case "2"

              ocat.Create("Provider=Microsoft.Jet.OLEDB.4.0;Jet
OLEDB:Engine Type=3;Data Source=" & Filename)
```

```vb
        Case "3"

                ocat.Create("Provider=Microsoft.Jet.OLEDB.4.0;Jet
OLEDB:Engine Type=4;Data Source=" & Filename)

        Case "4"

                ocat.Create("Provider=Microsoft.Jet.OLEDB.4.0;Jet
OLEDB:Engine Type=5;Data Source=" & Filename)


    End Select

End Sub
```

Create Database And Create Table

```vb
Public Sub Create_Database_And_Create_Table(ByVal Filename As String,
                    ByVal Tablename As String,
                    ByVal fNames() As string,
                    ByVal fTypes() As string,
                    ByVal fSizes() As string,
                    ByVal Version As String)

    Dim ocat As Object = CreateObject("ADOX.Catalog")

    Select Case Version

        Case "1"

                ocat.Create("Provider=Microsoft.Jet.OLEDB.4.0;Jet
OLEDB:Engine Type=1;Data Source=" & Filename)


        Case "11"

                ocat.Create("Provider=Microsoft.Jet.OLEDB.4.0;Jet
OLEDB:Engine Type=2;Data Source=" & Filename)
```

```
        Case "2"

                ocat.Create("Provider=Microsoft.Jet.OLEDB.4.0;Jet
OLEDB:Engine Type=3;Data Source=" & Filename)


        Case "3"

                ocat.Create("Provider=Microsoft.Jet.OLEDB.4.0;Jet
OLEDB:Engine Type=4;Data Source=" & Filename)

        Case "4"

                ocat.Create("Provider=Microsoft.Jet.OLEDB.4.0;Jet
OLEDB:Engine Type=5;Data Source=" & Filename)


    End Select

Dim oTable as Object = CreateObject("ADOX.Table")
oTable.Name = Tablename
For x = 0 To Ubound(fNames) - 1
    If fTypes(x) <> "203" then
        oTable.Columns.Append(fNames(x), fTypes(x), fSizes(x))
    else
        oTable.Columns.Append(fNames(x), fTypes(x))
    End If
Next
ocat.Tables.Append(oTable)
oTable = Nothing
ocat = Nothing

End Sub
```

Create Database, Create and Populate Table

```
Public Sub Create_Database_Create_Table_And_Populate_Table(ByVal Filename
As String,    ByVal Tablename As String,    ByVal fNames() As String,
```

```
ByVal fTypes() As String,   ByVal fSizes() As String, ByVal fValues(,) As String,
ByVal Version As String)


    Dim ocat As Object = CreateObject("ADOX.Catalog")

    Select Case Version

      Case "1"

                    ocat.Create("Provider=Microsoft.Jet.OLEDB.4.0;Jet OLEDB:Engine
Type=1;Data Source=" & Filename)


      Case "11"

                    ocat.Create("Provider=Microsoft.Jet.OLEDB.4.0;Jet OLEDB:Engine
Type=2;Data Source=" & Filename)


        Case "2"

                    ocat.Create("Provider=Microsoft.Jet.OLEDB.4.0;Jet OLEDB:Engine
Type=3;Data Source=" & Filename)


        Case "3"

                    ocat.Create("Provider=Microsoft.Jet.OLEDB.4.0;Jet OLEDB:Engine
Type=4;Data Source=" & Filename)

        Case "4"

                    ocat.Create("Provider=Microsoft.Jet.OLEDB.4.0;Jet OLEDB:Engine
Type=5;Data Source=" & Filename)


    End Select
Dim oTable as Object = CreateObject("ADOX.Table")
oTable.Name = Tablename
For x = 0 To Ubound(fNames) − 1
   If fTypes(x) <> "203" then
     oTable.Columns.Append(fNames(x), fTypes(x), fSizes(x))
   else
     oTable.Columns.Append(fNames(x), fTypes(x))
   End If
Next
ocat.Tables.Append(oTable)
```

```
oTable = Nothing
ocat = Nothing

Dim rs As Object = CreateObject("ADODB.Recordset")
rs.ActiveConnection = "Provider=Microsoft.Jet.OLEDB.4.0;Data Source=" & filename
& ";"
rs.CursorLocation = 3
rs.LockType = 3
rs.Source = "Select * From [" & tablename & "]"
rs.Open()

For y as Integer = 0 to Values.GetLength(0) -1
  rs.AddNew()
  For x = 0 To Names.GetLength(0)- 1
    rs.Fields(x).Value = Values(y,x)
  Next
  rs.Update()
Next

End Sub
```

Create Database, Create and Populate Table, Return Recordset

```
    Public  Function  CDatabase_CTable_PTable_And_RRecordset(ByVal  Filename  As
String,
                         ByVal Tablename As String,
                         ByVal fNames() As String,
                         ByVal fTypes() As String,
                         ByVal fSizes() As String,
                         ByVal fValues(,) As String,
                         ByVal Version As String) As Object

    Dim ocat As Object = CreateObject("ADOX.Catalog")

    Select Case Version

      Case "1"

                    ocat.Create("Provider=Microsoft.Jet.OLEDB.4.0;Jet OLEDB:Engine
Type=1;Data Source=" & Filename)
```

```
        Case "11"

                ocat.Create("Provider=Microsoft.Jet.OLEDB.4.0;Jet OLEDB:Engine
Type=2;Data Source=" & Filename)


        Case "2"

                ocat.Create("Provider=Microsoft.Jet.OLEDB.4.0;Jet OLEDB:Engine
Type=3;Data Source=" & Filename)


        Case "3"

                ocat.Create("Provider=Microsoft.Jet.OLEDB.4.0;Jet OLEDB:Engine
Type=4;Data Source=" & Filename)


        Case "4"

                ocat.Create("Provider=Microsoft.Jet.OLEDB.4.0;Jet OLEDB:Engine
Type=5;Data Source=" & Filename)


    End Select

Dim oTable as Object = CreateObject("ADOX.Table")
oTable.Name = Tablename
For x = 0 To Ubound(fNames) - 1
   If fTypes(x) <> "203" then
     oTable.Columns.Append(fNames(x), fTypes(x), fSizes(x))
   else
     oTable.Columns.Append(fNames(x), fTypes(x))
   End If
Next
ocat.Tables.Append(oTable)
oTable = Nothing
ocat = Nothing

Dim rs As Object = CreateObject("ADODB.Recordset")
rs.ActiveConnection = "Provider=Microsoft.Jet.OLEDB.4.0;Data Source=" & filename
& ";"
rs.CursorLocation = 3
rs.LockType = 3
rs.Source = "Select * From [" & tablename & "]"
rs.Open()
```

```
For y as Integer = 0 to Values.GetLength(0) -1
    rs.AddNew()
    For x = 0 To Names.GetLength(0)- 1
        rs.Fields(x).Value = Values(y,x)
    Next
    rs.Update()
Next

return rs

End Function
```

Open Database and Create Table

```
Public Sub OpenDatabase_CTable(ByVal Filename As String, ByVal Tablename As
String,  ByVal fNames() As String,  ByVal fTypes() As String,   ByVal fSizes() As
String)


Dim cn as Object = CreateObject("ADODB.Connection")
Cn.ConnectionString = "Provider=Microsoft.Jet.OleDb.4.0;Data Source=" & filename
& ";"
Cn.Open()

Dim ocat as Object = CreateObject("ADOX.Catalog")
ocat.ActiveConnection = cn

Dim oTable as Object = CreateObject("ADOX.Table")
oTable.Name = Tablename
For x = 0 To Ubound(fNames) – 1
    If fTypes(x) <> "203" then
        oTable.Columns.Append(fNames(x), fTypes(x), fSizes(x))
    else
        oTable.Columns.Append(fNames(x), fTypes(x))
    End If
Next
ocat.Tables.Append(oTable)
oTable = Nothing
ocat = Nothing
```

End Sub

Open Database, Create and Populate Table, Return Recordset


```
  Public Function OpenDatabase_CTable_PTable_Return_Recordset(ByVal Filename
As String, ByVal Tablename As String, ByVal fNames() As String,
ByVal fTypes() As String,  ByVal fSizes() As String, ByVal fValues(,) As String) As
Object


Dim cn as Object = CreateObject("ADODB.Connection")
Cn.ConnectionString = "Provider=Microsoft.Jet.OleDb.4.0;Data Source=" & filename
& ";"
Cn.Open()

Dim ocat as Object = CreateObject("ADOX.Catalog")
ocat.ActiveConnection = cn

Dim oTable as Object = CreateObject("ADOX.Table")
oTable.Name = Tablename
For x = 0 To Ubound(fNames) - 1
   If fTypes(x) <> "203" then
     oTable.Columns.Append(fNames(x), fTypes(x), fSizes(x))
   else
     oTable.Columns.Append(fNames(x), fTypes(x))
   End If
Next
ocat.Tables.Append(oTable)
oTable = Nothing
ocat = Nothing


For x as Integer = 0 To fNames.GetLength(0)-1
        Dim fld As Object = Nothing
        If fTypes(x) = "12" then
          fld = tbldef.CreateField(fNames(x), fTypes(x))
        else
          fld = tbldef.CreateField(fNames(x), fTypes(x), fSizes(x))
        End If
        fld.AllowZeroLength = True
```

```
            tbldef.Fields.Append(fld)
        Next
        db.TableDefs.Append(tbldef)

        Dim rs as Object = db.OpenRecordset(Tablename)

        For y as Integer = 0 To fValues.GetLength(0)-1
            rs.AddNew()
            For x as Integer = 0 To fNames.GetLength(0)-1
                rs.Fields(fNames(x)).Value = fValues(y, x)
            Next
            rs.UpDate()
        Next
        return rs
    End Sub
```

Open Database and Populate Table

```
    Public Sub OpenDatabase_PTable(ByVal Filename As String, ByVal Tablename As
String,  ByVal fValues(,) As String)

Dim cn as Object = CreateObject("ADODB.Connection")
Cn.ConnectionString = "Provider=Microsoft.Jet.OleDb.4.0;Data Source=" & filename
& ";"
Cn.Open()

Dim rs as Object = CreateObject("ADODB.Recordset")
Rs.ActiveConnection = cn
Rs.CursorLocation = 3
Rs.Locktype = 3
Rs.Open("Select * from [" & Tablename & "])
For y as Integer = 0 To fValues.GetLength(0)-1
    rs.AddNew()
    For x as Integer = 0 To fNames.GetLength(0)-1
        rs.Fields(fNames(x)).Value = fValues(y, x)
    Next
    rs.UpDate()
Next
```

End Sub

Open Database, Populate Table and Return Recordset

```
Public Function OpenDatabase_PTable_Return_Recordset(ByVal Filename As
String, ByVal Tablename As String, ByVal fValues(,) As String) As Object

Dim cn as Object = CreateObject("ADODB.Connection")
Cn.ConnectionString = "Provider=Microsoft.Jet.OleDb.4.0;Data Source=" & filename
& ";"
Cn.Open()

Dim rs as Object = CreateObject("ADODB.Recordset")
Rs.ActiveConnection = cn
Rs.CursorLocation = 3
Rs.Locktype = 3
Rs.Open("Select * from [" & Tablename & "])
For y as Integer = 0 To fValues.GetLength(0)-1
    rs.AddNew()
    For x as Integer = 0 To fNames.GetLength(0)-1
      rs.Fields(fNames(x)).Value = fValues(y, x)
    Next
    rs.UpDate()
Next


    return rs

End Function
```

Open Database and Return Recordset

```
Public Function OpenDatabase_Return_Recordset(ByVal Filename As String,
          ByVal Tablename As String) As Object


Dim cn as Object = CreateObject("ADODB.Connection")
```

```
Cn.ConnectionString = "Provider=Microsoft.Jet.OleDb.4.0;Data Source=" & filename
& ";"
Cn.Open()

Dim rs as Object = CreateObject("ADODB.Recordset")
rs.ActiveConnection = cn
rs.CursorLocation = 3
rs.Locktype = 3
rs.Open("Select * from [" & Tablename & "])

return rs

End Function
```

ODBC

Opening, Creating and Populating Tables

While we may not be able to create Access Tables with ODBC, we can certainly connect, create and populate tables and return recordsets.

Open Database and Create Table

Public Sub Open_Database_An_CreateTable_Using_ODBC(ByVal Filename as String, ByVal Tablename As String, ByVal fNames() as String, ByVal fTypes() As String, ByVal fSizes() As String)

```
    Dim tempstr As String = "CREATE TABLE " & Tablename & "("
    Dim tstr As String = ""

    For x As Integer = 0 To fNames.GetLength(0)-1
      If tstr <> "" then
        tstr = tstr & ","
      End If
      If fSizes(x) <> "" then
        tstr = tstr & fNames(x) & " " & fTypes(x) & "(" & fSizes(x) &
")"
      else
        tstr = tstr & fNames(x) & " " & fTypes(x) & " "
      End If

    Next
```

```vbnet
        tempstr = tempstr & tstr & ")"


        Dim cn As OdbcConnection = New OdbcConnection()
        cn.ConnectionString = "Driver={Microsoft Access Driver
(*.mdb)}; dbq=" & filename & ";"
        cn.Open()

        Dim cmd As OdbcCommand = New OdbcCommand()
        cmd.Connection = cn
        cmd.CommandType = CommandType.Text
        cmd.CommandText = tempstr
        cmd.ExecuteNonQuery()
```

Open Database, Create and Populate Table Using a DataSet

Public Sub Open_Database_An_CreateTable_Using_ODBC(ByVal Filename as String, ByVal Tablename As String, ByVal fNames() as String, ByVal fTypes() As String, ByVal fSizes() As String)

```vbnet
        Dim tempstr As String = "CREATE TABLE " & Tablename & "("
        Dim tstr As String = ""
```

For x As Integer = 0 To fNames.GetLength(0)-1

```vbnet
          If tstr <> "" then
            tstr = tstr & ","
          End If
          If fSizes(x) <> "" then
            tstr = tstr & fNames(x) & " " & fTypes(x) & "(" & fSizes(x) &
")"
```

else

```vbnet
            tstr = tstr & fNames(x) & " " & fTypes(x) & " "
```

End If

Next

```vbnet
        tempstr = tempstr & tstr & ")"
```

```
    Dim cn As OdbcConnection = New OdbcConnection()
    cn.ConnectionString = "Driver={Microsoft Access Driver
(*.mdb)}; dbq=" & filename & ";"
    cn.Open()

    Dim cmd As OdbcCommand = New OdbcCommand()
    cmd.Connection = cn
    cmd.CommandType = CommandType.Text
    cmd.CommandText = tempstr
    cmd.ExecuteNonQuery()

    Dim da As OdbcDataAdapter = New OdbcDataAdapter(cmd)
    Dim cb As OdbcCommandBuilder = New OdbcCommandBuilder(da)
    da.MissingSchemaAction = MissingSchemaAction.AddWithKey
    Dim ds As System.Data.DataSet = New System.Data.DataSet
    da.Fill(ds)

    For y = 0 To Values.GetLength(0) - 1
        Dim nr As System.Data.DataRow = ds.Tables(0).NewRow
        For x = 0 To Names.GetLength(0) - 1
            nr.Item(Names(x)) = Values(y, x)
        Next
        ds.Tables(0).Rows.Add(nr)
        ds.Tables(0).AcceptChanges()
    Next
```

Open Database, Create and Populate Table Using a DataTable

```
    Public Sub Open_Database_An_CreateTable_Using_ODBC(ByVal Filename as
String, ByVal Tablename As String, ByVal fNames() as String, ByVal fTypes() As
String, ByVal fSizes() As String)

    Dim tempstr As String = "CREATE TABLE " & Tablename & "("
    Dim tstr As String = ""

    For x As Integer = 0 To fNames.GetLength(0)-1
      If tstr <> "" then
        tstr = tstr & ","
      End If
      If fSizes(x) <> "" then
```

```vbnet
            tstr = tstr & fNames(x) & " " & fTypes(x) & "(" & fSizes(x) &
")"
        else
            tstr = tstr & fNames(x) & " " & fTypes(x) & " "

        End If

    Next

    tempstr = tempstr & tstr & ")"

    Dim cn As OdbcConnection = New OdbcConnection()
    cn.ConnectionString = "Driver={Microsoft Access Driver
(*.mdb)}; dbq=" & filename & ";"
    cn.Open()

    Dim cmd As OdbcCommand = New OdbcCommand()
    cmd.Connection = cn
    cmd.CommandType = CommandType.Text
    cmd.CommandText = tempstr
    cmd.ExecuteNonQuery()

    Dim da As OdbcDataAdapter = New OdbcDataAdapter(cmd)
    Dim cb As OdbcCommandBuilder = New OdbcCommandBuilder(da)
    da.MissingSchemaAction = MissingSchemaAction.AddWithKey
    Dim dt As System.Data.DataTable = New System.Data.DataTable
    da.Fill(dt)

    For y = 0 To Values.GetLength(0) - 1
        Dim nr As System.Data.DataRow = dt.NewRow
        For x = 0 To Names.GetLength(0) - 1
            nr.Item(Names(x)) = Values(y, x)
        Next
        dt.Rows.Add(nr)
        dt.AcceptChanges()
    Next

    End Sub
```

Open Database, Create and Populate Table Using a DataView

```vb
Public Sub Open_Database_An_CreateTable_Using_ODBC(ByVal Filename as
String, ByVal Tablename As String, ByVal fNames() as String, ByVal fTypes() As
String, ByVal fSizes() As String)

    Dim tempstr As String = "CREATE TABLE " & Tablename & "("
    Dim tstr As String = ""

    For x As Integer = 0 To fNames.GetLength(0)-1
      If tstr <> "" then
        tstr = tstr & ","
      End If
      If fSizes(x) <> "" then
        tstr = tstr & fNames(x) & " " & fTypes(x) & "(" & fSizes(x) &
")"
      else
        tstr = tstr & fNames(x) & " " & fTypes(x) & " "

      End If

    Next

    tempstr = tempstr & tstr & ")"

    Dim cn As OdbcConnection = New OdbcConnection()
    cn.ConnectionString = "Driver={Microsoft Access Driver
(*.mdb)}; dbq=" & filename & ";"
    cn.Open()

    Dim cmd As OdbcCommand = New OdbcCommand()
    cmd.Connection = cn
    cmd.CommandType = CommandType.Text
    cmd.CommandText = tempstr
    cmd.ExecuteNonQuery()

    Dim da As OdbcDataAdapter = New OdbcDataAdapter(cmd)
    Dim cb As OdbcCommandBuilder = New OdbcCommandBuilder(da)
    da.MissingSchemaAction = MissingSchemaAction.AddWithKey
    Dim dt As System.Data.DataTable = New System.Data.DataTable
    da.Fill(dt)

    Dim dv As System.Data.DataView = dt.DefaultView()
```

```
    For y = 0 To Values.GetLength(0) - 1
        Dim nr As System.Data.DataRow = dv.Table.NewRow
        For x = 0 To Names.GetLength(0) - 1
            nr.Item(Names(x)) = Values(y, x)
        Next
        dv.Table.Rows.Add(nr)
        dv.Table.AcceptChanges()
    Next
```

End sub

Open Database, Create and Populate Table And Return DataSet

Public Function Open_Database_CreateTable_Using_ODBC(ByVal Filename as String, ByVal Tablename As String, ByVal fNames() as String, ByVal fTypes() As String, ByVal fSizes() As String) As System.Data.DataSet

```
    Dim tempstr As String = "CREATE TABLE " & Tablename & "("
    Dim tstr As String = ""
```

For x As Integer = 0 To fNames.GetLength(0)-1
    If tstr <> "" then
        tstr = tstr & ","
    End If
    If fSizes(x) <> "" then
        tstr = tstr & fNames(x) & " " & fTypes(x) & "(" & fSizes(x) &
")"
    else
        tstr = tstr & fNames(x) & " " & fTypes(x) & " "
    End If

Next

tempstr = tempstr & tstr & ")"

```
    Dim cn As OdbcConnection = New OdbcConnection()
```

```
        cn.ConnectionString = "Driver={Microsoft Access Driver
(*.mdb)}; dbq=" & filename & ";"
        cn.Open()

        Dim cmd As OdbcCommand = New OdbcCommand()
        cmd.Connection = cn
        cmd.CommandType = CommandType.Text
        cmd.CommandText = tempstr
        cmd.ExecuteNonQuery()

        Dim da As OdbcDataAdapter = New OdbcDataAdapter(cmd)
        Dim cb As OdbcCommandBuilder = New OdbcCommandBuilder(da)
        da.MissingSchemaAction = MissingSchemaAction.AddWithKey
        Dim ds As System.Data.DataSet = New System.Data.DataSet
        da.Fill(ds)

        For y = 0 To Values.GetLength(0) - 1
            Dim nr As System.Data.DataRow = ds.Tables(0).NewRow
            For x = 0 To Names.GetLength(0) - 1
                nr.Item(Names(x)) = Values(y, x)
            Next
            ds.Tables(0).Rows.Add(nr)
            ds.Tables(0).AcceptChanges()
        Next

        Return ds

    End Function
```

Open Database, Create and Populate Table And Return A DataTable

Public function Open_Database_An_CreateTable_Using_ODBC(ByVal Filename as String, ByVal Tablename As String, ByVal fNames() as String, ByVal fTypes() As String, ByVal fSizes() As String) As System.Data.DataTable

```
        Dim tempstr As String = "CREATE TABLE " & Tablename & "("
        Dim tstr As String = ""

        For x As Integer = 0 To fNames.GetLength(0)-1
          If tstr <> "" then
            tstr = tstr & ","
          End If
```

```vbnet
        If fSizes(x) <> "" then
            tstr = tstr & fNames(x) & "  " & fTypes(x) & "(" & fSizes(x) &
")"

        else
            tstr = tstr & fNames(x) & "  " & fTypes(x) & " "

        End If

    Next


    tempstr = tempstr & tstr & ")"


    Dim cn As OdbcConnection = New OdbcConnection()
    cn.ConnectionString = "Driver={Microsoft Access Driver
(*.mdb)}; dbq=" & filename & ";"
    cn.Open()

    Dim cmd As OdbcCommand = New OdbcCommand()
    cmd.Connection = cn
    cmd.CommandType = CommandType.Text
    cmd.CommandText = tempstr
    cmd.ExecuteNonQuery()

    Dim da As OdbcDataAdapter = New OdbcDataAdapter(cmd)
    Dim cb As OdbcCommandBuilder = New OdbcCommandBuilder(da)
    da.MissingSchemaAction = MissingSchemaAction.AddWithKey
    Dim dt As System.Data.DataTable = New System.Data.DataTable
    da.Fill(dt)

    For y = 0 To Values.GetLength(0) - 1
        Dim nr As System.Data.DataRow = dt.NewRow
        For x = 0 To Names.GetLength(0) - 1
            nr.Item(Names(x)) = Values(y, x)
        Next
        dt.Rows.Add(nr)
        dt.AcceptChanges()
    Next

    Return dt
End Function
```

Open Database, Create and Populate Table and Return a DataView

Public Function Open_Database_An_CreateTable_Using_ODBC(ByVal Filename as String, ByVal Tablename As String, ByVal fNames() as String, ByVal fTypes() As String, ByVal fSizes() As String) As System.Data.DataView

```
Dim tempstr As String = "CREATE TABLE " & Tablename & "("
Dim tstr As String = ""

For x As Integer = 0 To fNames.GetLength(0)-1
  If tstr <> "" then
    tstr = tstr & ","
  End If
  If fSizes(x) <> "" then
    tstr = tstr & fNames(x) & " " & fTypes(x) & "(" & fSizes(x) &
")"
  else
    tstr = tstr & fNames(x) & " " & fTypes(x) & " "
  End If

Next

tempstr = tempstr & tstr & ")"

Dim cn As OdbcConnection = New OdbcConnection()
cn.ConnectionString = "Driver={Microsoft Access Driver
(*.mdb)}; dbq=" & filename & ";"
cn.Open()

Dim cmd As OdbcCommand = New OdbcCommand()
cmd.Connection = cn
cmd.CommandType = CommandType.Text
cmd.CommandText = tempstr
cmd.ExecuteNonQuery()

Dim da As OdbcDataAdapter = New OdbcDataAdapter(cmd)
Dim cb As OdbcCommandBuilder = New OdbcCommandBuilder(da)
da.MissingSchemaAction = MissingSchemaAction.AddWithKey
Dim dt As System.Data.DataTable = New System.Data.DataTable
```

```
da.Fill(dt)

Dim dv As System.Data.DataView = dt.DefaultView()

For y = 0 To Values.GetLength(0) - 1
    Dim nr As System.Data.DataRow = dv.Table.NewRow
    For x = 0 To Names.GetLength(0) - 1
        nr.Item(Names(x)) = Values(y, x)
    Next
    dv.Table.Rows.Add(nr)
    dv.Table.AcceptChanges()
Next

Return dv

End sub
```

ADO AND OLEDB

Mention ADO and OLEDB in the same sentence and you're most like going to get stares like you've lost your marbles.

As for me, it is probably warranted.

Fact is, OleDb's DataAdapter takes an ADO Recordset and coverts it with your help to a DataSet or DataTable. You add the code to include the DataView.

Question is, why would you want to convert your ADO Recordset to a Dataset or DataTable? Well, for one thing, three lines of code buys you the ability to dynamically bind the DataSet, DataTable or DataView to things like the DataGridView in the IDE and DataGridView and ListView used in WPF.

So, let's take the AODX\ADO code examples and add to the ones that return a recordset and add the OleDb code.

Create Database, Create and Populate Table and Populate A Dataset

```
Public Sub CDatabase_CTable_PTable_And_RRecordset(ByVal Filename As String,
                    ByVal Tablename As String,
                    ByVal fNames() As String,
                    ByVal fTypes() As String,
                    ByVal fSizes() As String,
                    ByVal fValues(,) As String,
                    ByVal Version As String)

    Dim ocat As Object = CreateObject("ADOX.Catalog")

    Select Case Version

        Case "1"
```

```
        ocat.Create("Provider=Microsoft.Jet.OLEDB.4.0;Jet OLEDB:Engine
Type=1;Data Source=" & Filename)


    Case "11"

        ocat.Create("Provider=Microsoft.Jet.OLEDB.4.0;Jet OLEDB:Engine
Type=2;Data Source=" & Filename)


    Case "2"

        ocat.Create("Provider=Microsoft.Jet.OLEDB.4.0;Jet OLEDB:Engine
Type=3;Data Source=" & Filename)


    Case "3"

        ocat.Create("Provider=Microsoft.Jet.OLEDB.4.0;Jet OLEDB:Engine
Type=4;Data Source=" & Filename)

    Case "4"

        ocat.Create("Provider=Microsoft.Jet.OLEDB.4.0;Jet OLEDB:Engine
Type=5;Data Source=" & Filename)


    End Select

Dim oTable as Object = CreateObject("ADOX.Table")
oTable.Name = Tablename
For x = 0 To Ubound(fNames) - 1
    If fTypes(x) <> "203" then
        oTable.Columns.Append(fNames(x), fTypes(x), fSizes(x))
    else
        oTable.Columns.Append(fNames(x), fTypes(x))
    End If
Next
ocat.Tables.Append(oTable)
oTable = Nothing
ocat = Nothing

Dim rs As Object = CreateObject("ADODB.Recordset")
rs.ActiveConnection = "Provider=Microsoft.Jet.OLEDB.4.0;Data Source=" & filename
& ";"
rs.CursorLocation = 3
rs.LockType = 3
rs.Source = "Select * From [" & tablename & "]"
```

```
rs.Open()

For y as Integer = 0 to Values.GetLength(0) -1
  rs.AddNew()
  For x = 0 To Names.GetLength(0)- 1
    rs.Fields(x).Value = Values(y,x)
  Next
  rs.Update()
Next

Dim da as new System.Data.OleDb.OleDbDataAdapter
Dim ds as new System.Data.DataSet
Da.Fill(ds, rs, tablename)



End sub
```

Create Database, Create and Populate Table and Populate A DataTable

```
Public Sub CDatabase_CTable_PTable_And_RRecordset(ByVal Filename As String,
                    ByVal Tablename As String,
                    ByVal fNames() As String,
                    ByVal fTypes() As String,
                    ByVal fSizes() As String,
                    ByVal fValues(,) As String,
                    ByVal Version As String)

    Dim ocat As Object = CreateObject("ADOX.Catalog")

    Select Case Version

      Case "1"

           ocat.Create("Provider=Microsoft.Jet.OLEDB.4.0;Jet OLEDB:Engine
Type=1;Data Source=" & Filename)


      Case "11"
```

```
        ocat.Create("Provider=Microsoft.Jet.OLEDB.4.0;Jet OLEDB:Engine
Type=2;Data Source=" & Filename)


    Case "2"

        ocat.Create("Provider=Microsoft.Jet.OLEDB.4.0;Jet OLEDB:Engine
Type=3;Data Source=" & Filename)


    Case "3"

        ocat.Create("Provider=Microsoft.Jet.OLEDB.4.0;Jet OLEDB:Engine
Type=4;Data Source=" & Filename)

    Case "4"

        ocat.Create("Provider=Microsoft.Jet.OLEDB.4.0;Jet OLEDB:Engine
Type=5;Data Source=" & Filename)


    End Select

Dim oTable as Object = CreateObject("ADOX.Table")
oTable.Name = Tablename
For x = 0 To Ubound(fNames) - 1
    If fTypes(x) <> "203" then
        oTable.Columns.Append(fNames(x), fTypes(x), fSizes(x))
    else
        oTable.Columns.Append(fNames(x), fTypes(x))
    End If
Next
ocat.Tables.Append(oTable)
oTable = Nothing
ocat = Nothing

Dim rs As Object = CreateObject("ADODB.Recordset")
rs.ActiveConnection = "Provider=Microsoft.Jet.OLEDB.4.0;Data Source=" & filename
& ";"
rs.CursorLocation = 3
rs.LockType = 3
rs.Source = "Select * From [" & tablename & "]"
rs.Open()

For y as Integer = 0 to Values.GetLength(0) -1
    rs.AddNew()
```

```
      For x = 0 To Names.GetLength(0)- 1
         rs.Fields(x).Value = Values(y,x)
      Next
      rs.Update()
Next

Dim da as new System.Data.OleDb.OleDbDataAdapter
Dim dt as new System.Data.DataTable
Da.Fill(dt, rs)

End Sub
```

Create Database, Create and Populate Table and Populate A DataView

```
Public Sub CDatabase_CTable_PTable_And_RRecordset(ByVal Filename As String,
                      ByVal Tablename As String,
                      ByVal fNames() As String,
                      ByVal fTypes() As String,
                      ByVal fSizes() As String,
                      ByVal fValues(,) As String,
                      ByVal Version As String)

   Dim ocat As Object = CreateObject("ADOX.Catalog")

   Select Case Version

     Case "1"

          ocat.Create("Provider=Microsoft.Jet.OLEDB.4.0;Jet OLEDB:Engine
Type=1;Data Source=" & Filename)

     Case "11"

          ocat.Create("Provider=Microsoft.Jet.OLEDB.4.0;Jet OLEDB:Engine
Type=2;Data Source=" & Filename)

     Case "2"
```

```
        ocat.Create("Provider=Microsoft.Jet.OLEDB.4.0;Jet OLEDB:Engine
Type=3;Data Source=" & Filename)


    Case "3"

        ocat.Create("Provider=Microsoft.Jet.OLEDB.4.0;Jet OLEDB:Engine
Type=4;Data Source=" & Filename)

    Case "4"

        ocat.Create("Provider=Microsoft.Jet.OLEDB.4.0;Jet OLEDB:Engine
Type=5;Data Source=" & Filename)


    End Select

Dim oTable as Object = CreateObject("ADOX.Table")
oTable.Name = Tablename
For x = 0 To Ubound(fNames) − 1
    If fTypes(x) <> "203" then
        oTable.Columns.Append(fNames(x), fTypes(x), fSizes(x))
    else
        oTable.Columns.Append(fNames(x), fTypes(x))
    End If
Next
ocat.Tables.Append(oTable)
oTable = Nothing
ocat = Nothing

Dim rs As Object = CreateObject("ADODB.Recordset")
rs.ActiveConnection = "Provider=Microsoft.Jet.OLEDB.4.0;Data Source=" & filename
& ";"
rs.CursorLocation = 3
rs.LockType = 3
rs.Source = "Select * From [" & tablename & "]"
rs.Open()

For y as Integer = 0 to Values.GetLength(0) −1
    rs.AddNew()
    For x = 0 To Names.GetLength(0)− 1
        rs.Fields(x).Value = Values(y,x)
    Next
    rs.Update()
Next
```

```
Dim da as new System.Data.OleDb.OleDbDataAdapter
Dim dt as new System.Data.DataTable
Da.Fill(dt, rs)
Dim dv as System.Data.DataView = dt.DefaultView

End Sub
```

Open Database, Populate Table and Populate DataSet

```
   Public Sub OpenDatabase_PTable(ByVal Filename As String, ByVal Tablename As
String,  ByVal fValues(,) As String)

Dim cn as Object = CreateObject("ADODB.Connection")
Cn.ConnectionString = "Provider=Microsoft.Jet.OleDb.4.0;Data Source=" & filename
& ";"
Cn.Open()

Dim rs as Object = CreateObject("ADODB.Recordset")
Rs.ActiveConnection = cn
Rs.CursorLocation = 3
Rs.Locktype = 3
Rs.Open("Select * from [" & Tablename & "])
For y as Integer = 0 To fValues.GetLength(0)-1
    rs.AddNew()
    For x as Integer = 0 To fNames.GetLength(0)-1
      rs.Fields(fNames(x)).Value = fValues(y, x)
    Next
    rs.UpDate()
  Next

Dim da as new System.Data.OleDb.OleDbDataAdapter
Dim ds as new System.Data.DataSet
Da.Fill(ds, rs, tablename)


End Sub
```

Open Database, Populate Table and Populate a DataTable

```
    Public Sub OpenDatabase_PTable(ByVal Filename As String, ByVal Tablename As
String, ByVal fValues(,) As String)t

Dim cn as Object = CreateObject("ADODB.Connection")
Cn.ConnectionString = "Provider=Microsoft.Jet.OleDb.4.0;Data Source=" & filename
& ";"
Cn.Open()

Dim rs as Object = CreateObject("ADODB.Recordset")
Rs.ActiveConnection = cn
Rs.CursorLocation = 3
Rs.Locktype = 3
Rs.Open("Select * from [" & Tablename & "])
For y as Integer = 0 To fValues.GetLength(0)-1
    rs.AddNew()
    For x as Integer = 0 To fNames.GetLength(0)-1
      rs.Fields(fNames(x)).Value = fValues(y, x)
    Next
    rs.UpDate()
 Next

Dim da as new System.Data.OleDb.OleDbDataAdapter
Dim dt as new System.Data.DataTable
Da.Fill(dt, rs)

End Sub
```

Open Database, Populate Table and Populate a DataView

```
    Public Sub OpenDatabase_PTable(ByVal Filename As String, ByVal Tablename As
String, ByVal fValues(,) As String)t

Dim cn as Object = CreateObject("ADODB.Connection")
Cn.ConnectionString = "Provider=Microsoft.Jet.OleDb.4.0;Data Source=" & filename
& ";"
```

```vbnet
Cn.Open()

Dim rs as Object = CreateObject("ADODB.Recordset")
Rs.ActiveConnection = cn
Rs.CursorLocation = 3
Rs.Locktype = 3
Rs.Open("Select * from [" & Tablename & "])
For y as Integer = 0 To fValues.GetLength(0)-1
    rs.AddNew()
    For x as Integer = 0 To fNames.GetLength(0)-1
      rs.Fields(fNames(x)).Value = fValues(y, x)
    Next
    rs.UpDate()
 Next

Dim da as new System.Data.OleDb.OleDbDataAdapter
Dim dt as new System.Data.DataTable
Da.Fill(dt, rs)

Dim dv as System.Data.DataView = dt.DefaultView

End Sub
```

ODBC STAND ALONE CODE

When I decided to write this book, I had no Idea how much work would go into all the variety of ways you can connect and work with Access Databases. Yes, I knew there was more than one way to do it. But being here, on page 85 and knowing how many examples are coming your way, it is still hard for me to believe that it is going to come very close to 100 pages. WOW!

So, below, are coding examples that are pretty much standard stock and usable.

ODBC Connection, Command and DataAdapter Using a Dataset

Public Sub Connect_To_Access_Database_using_ODBC_And_DataSet(ByVal cnstr as String, ByVal strQuery As String)

```
Dim cn As System.Data.Odbc.OdbcConnection  = new
System.Data.Odbc.OdbcConnection(cnstr)
cn.Open()

    Dim cmd As System.Data.Odbc.OdbcCommand  = new
    System.Data.Odbc.OdbcCommand()
    cmd.Connection = cn
    cmd.CommandType = 1
    cmd.CommandText = strQuery
    cmd.ExecuteNonquery()

    Dim da As System.Data.Odbc.OdbcDataAdapter  = new
    System.Data.Odbc.OdbcDataAdapter(cmd)
    Dim ds as new System.Data.DataSet
    da.Fill(ds)
```

End Sub

ODBC Connection, Command and DataAdapter Using a DataTable

Public Sub Connect_To_Access_Database_using_ODBC_And_DataTable(ByVal cnstr as String, ByVal strQuery As String)

```
Dim cn As System.Data.Odbc.OdbcConnection   = new
System.Data.Odbc.OdbcConnection(cnstr)
cn.Open()

    Dim cmd As System.Data.Odbc.OdbcCommand   = new
    System.Data.Odbc.OdbcCommand()
    cmd.Connection = cn
    cmd.CommandType = 1
    cmd.CommandText = strQuery
    cmd.ExecuteNonquery()

    Dim da As System.Data.Odbc.OdbcDataAdapter   = new
    System.Data.Odbc.OdbcDataAdapter(cmd)
    Dim dt as new System.Data.DataTable
    da.Fill(dt)
```

End Sub

ODBC Connection, Command and DataAdapter Using a DataView

Public Sub Connect_To_Access_Database_using_ODBC_And_DataView(ByVal cnstr as String, ByVal strQuery As String)

```
Dim cn As System.Data.Odbc.OdbcConnection   = new
System.Data.Odbc.OdbcConnection(cnstr)
cn.Open()
```

```
Dim cmd As System.Data.Odbc.OdbcCommand   = new
System.Data.Odbc.OdbcCommand()
cmd.Connection = cn
cmd.CommandType = 1
cmd.CommandText = strQuery
cmd.ExecuteNonquery()

Dim da As System.Data.Odbc.OdbcDataAdapter   = new
System.Data.Odbc.OdbcDataAdapter(cmd)
Dim dt as new System.Data.DataTable
da.Fill(dt)
Dim dv as System.Data.DataView = dt.DefaultView
```

End Sub

ODBC Connection and DataAdapter Using a Dataset

Public   Sub   Connect_To_Access_Database_using_ODBC_And_DataSet(ByVal cnstr as String, ByVal strQuery As String)

```
Dim cn As System.Data.Odbc.OdbcConnection   = new
System.Data.Odbc.OdbcConnection(cnstr)
cn.Open()

Dim da As System.Data.Odbc.OdbcDataAdapter   = new
System.Data.Odbc.OdbcDataAdapter(strQuery, cn)
Dim ds as new System.Data.DataSet
da.Fill(ds)
```

End Sub

ODBC Connection and DataAdapter Using a DataTable

Public   Sub   Connect_To_Access_Database_using_ODBC_And_DataTable(ByVal cnstr as String, ByVal strQuery As String)

```
Dim cn As System.Data.Odbc.OdbcConnection   = new
System.Data.Odbc.OdbcConnection(cnstr)
cn.Open()

Dim da As System.Data.Odbc.OdbcDataAdapter   = new
System.Data.Odbc.OdbcDataAdapter(strQuery, cn)
Dim dt as new System.Data.DataTable
da.Fill(dt)


End Sub
```

ODBC Connection and DataAdapter Using a DataView

Public Sub Connect_To_Access_Database_using_ODBC_And_DataView(ByVal cnstr as String, ByVal strQuery As String)

```
Dim cn As System.Data.Odbc.OdbcConnection   = new
System.Data.Odbc.OdbcConnection(cnstr)
cn.Open()

Dim da As System.Data.Odbc.OdbcDataAdapter   = new
System.Data.Odbc.OdbcDataAdapter(strQuery, cn)
Dim dt as new System.Data.DataTable
da.Fill(dt)

Dim dv as System.Data.DataView = dt.DefaultView

End Sub
```

ODBC Command and DataAdapter Using a Dataset

Public Sub Connect_To_Access_Database_using_ODBC_And_DataSet(ByVal cnstr as String, ByVal strQuery As String)

```
Dim cmd As System.Data.Odbc.OdbcCommand   = new
System.Data.Odbc.OdbcCommand()
cmd.Connection = new System.Data.Odbc.OdbcConnection
cmd.Connection.ConnectionString = cnstr
cmd.Connection.Open()

cmd.CommandType = 1
cmd.CommandText = strQuery
cmd.ExecuteNonquery()

Dim da As System.Data.Odbc.OdbcDataAdapter  = new
System.Data.Odbc.OdbcDataAdapter(cmd)
Dim ds as new System.Data.DataSet
da.Fill(ds)


End Sub
```

ODBC Command and DataAdapter Using a DataTable

Public Sub Connect_To_Access_Database_using_ODBC_And_DataTable(ByVal cnstr as String, ByVal strQuery As String)

```
Dim cmd As System.Data.Odbc.OdbcCommand   = new
System.Data.Odbc.OdbcCommand()
cmd.Connection = new System.Data.Odbc.OdbcConnection
cmd.Connection.ConnectionString = cnstr
cmd.Connection.Open()

cmd.CommandType = 1
cmd.CommandText = strQuery
cmd.ExecuteNonquery()

Dim da As System.Data.Odbc.OdbcDataAdapter   = new
System.Data.Odbc.OdbcDataAdapter(cmd)
Dim dt as new System.Data.DataTable
da.Fill(dt)
```

```
End Sub
```

ODBC Command and DataAdapter Using a DataView

Public Sub Connect_To_Access_Database_using_ODBC_And_DataView(ByVal cnstr as String, ByVal strQuery As String)

```
Dim cmd As System.Data.Odbc.OdbcCommand  = new
System.Data.Odbc.OdbcCommand()
cmd.Connection = new System.Data.Odbc.OdbcConnection
cmd.Connection.ConnectionString = cnstr
cmd.Connection.Open()

cmd.CommandType = 1
cmd.CommandText = strQuery
cmd.ExecuteNonquery()

Dim da As System.Data.Odbc.OdbcDataAdapter  = new
System.Data.Odbc.OdbcDataAdapter(cmd)
Dim dt as new System.Data.DataTable
da.Fill(dt)
Dim dv as System.Data.DataView = dt.DefaultView
```

```
End Sub
```

ODBC DataAdapter Using a Dataset

Public Sub Connect_To_Access_Database_using_ODBC_And_DataSet(ByVal cnstr as String, ByVal strQuery As String)

```
Dim da As System.Data.Odbc.OdbcDataAdapter  = new
System.Data.Odbc.OdbcDataAdapter(strQuery, cnstr)
Dim ds as new System.Data.DataSet
```

```
        da.Fill(ds)


End Sub
```

ODBC DataAdapter Using a DataTable

Public Sub Connect_To_Access_Database_using_ODBC_And_DataTable(ByVal cnstr as String, ByVal strQuery As String)

```
        Dim da As System.Data.Odbc.OdbcDataAdapter  = new
        System.Data.Odbc.OdbcDataAdapter(strQuery, cnstr)
        Dim dt as new System.Data.DataTable
        da.Fill(dt)


End Sub
```

ODBC DataAdapter Using a DataView

Public Sub Connect_To_Access_Database_using_ODBC_And_DataView(ByVal cnstr as String, ByVal strQuery As String)

```
        Dim da As System.Data.Odbc.OdbcDataAdapter  = new
        System.Data.Odbc.OdbcDataAdapter(strQuery, cnstr)
        Dim dt as new System.Data.DataTable
        da.Fill(dt)
        Dim dv as System.Data.DataView = dt.DefaultView

End Sub
```

OLEDB

Stand Alone Code

If the truth were known – obviously, since I'm about to say it – it takes three lines of code to create and populate the OleDbDataAdapter:

```
Dim da as New System.Data.OleDb.OleDbDataAdapter(strQuery, cnstr)
Dim ds as new System.Data.DataSet
Da.Fill(ds)
```

It takes 2 to populate an ADODB.Recordset:

```
Dim rs as Object = CreateObject("ADODB.Recordset")
rs.Open(strQuery, cnstr)
```

Whether it is direct binding or dynamically driven non-binding, both gives you something to work with and get the job done. So, why bother with OleDb in the first place?

Simple, OLEDB is the easiest to work with.

OLEDB Connection, Command and DataAdapter Using a Dataset

Public Sub Connect_To_Access_Database_using_OLEDB_And_DataSet(ByVal cnstr as String, ByVal strQuery As String)

```
Dim cn As System.Data.OleDb.OleDbConnection   = new
System.Data.OleDb.OleDbConnection(cnstr)
```

```
cn.Open()

    Dim cmd As System.Data.OleDb.OleDbCommand   = new
    System.Data.OleDb.OleDbCommand()
    cmd.Connection = cn
    cmd.CommandType = 1
    cmd.CommandText = strQuery
    cmd.ExecuteNonquery()

    Dim da As System.Data.OleDb.OleDbDataAdapter   = new
    System.Data.OleDb.OleDbDataAdapter(cmd)
    Dim ds as new System.Data.DataSet
    da.Fill(ds)
```

End Sub

OLEDB Connection, Command and DataAdapter Using a DataTable

Public   Sub
Connect_To_Access_Database_using_OLEDB_And_DataTable(ByVal   cnstr   as
String, ByVal strQuery As String)

```
Dim cn As System.Data.OleDb.OleDbConnection   = new
System.Data.OleDb.OleDbConnection(cnstr)
cn.Open()

    Dim cmd As System.Data.OleDb.OleDbCommand   = new
    System.Data.OleDb.OleDbCommand()
    cmd.Connection = cn
    cmd.CommandType = 1
    cmd.CommandText = strQuery
    cmd.ExecuteNonquery()

    Dim da As System.Data.OleDb.OleDbDataAdapter   = new
    System.Data.OleDb.OleDbDataAdapter(cmd)
    Dim dt as new System.Data.DataTable
    da.Fill(dt)
```

End Sub

OLEDB Connection, Command and DataAdapter Using a DataView

Public Sub Connect_To_Access_Database_using_OLEDB_And_DataView(ByVal cnstr as String, ByVal strQuery As String)

```
Dim cn As System.Data.OleDb.OleDbConnection   = new
System.Data.OleDb.OleDbConnection(cnstr)
cn.Open()

    Dim cmd As System.Data.OleDb.OleDbCommand   = new
    System.Data.OleDb.OleDbCommand()
    cmd.Connection = cn
    cmd.CommandType = 1
    cmd.CommandText = strQuery
    cmd.ExecuteNonquery()

    Dim da As System.Data.OleDb.OleDbDataAdapter   = new
    System.Data.OleDb.OleDbDataAdapter(cmd)
    Dim dt as new System.Data.DataTable
    da.Fill(dt)
    Dim dv as System.Data.DataView = dt.DefaultView
```

End Sub

OLEDB Connection and DataAdapter Using a Dataset

Public Sub Connect_To_Access_Database_using_OLEDB_And_DataSet(ByVal cnstr as String, ByVal strQuery As String)

```
Dim cn As System.Data.OleDb.OleDbConnection   = new
System.Data.OleDb.OleDbConnection(cnstr)
cn.Open()

Dim da As System.Data.OleDb.OleDbDataAdapter   = new
System.Data.OleDb.OleDbDataAdapter(strQuery, cn)
  Dim ds as new System.Data.DataSet
  da.Fill(ds)
```

End Sub

OLEDB Connection and DataAdapter Using a DataTable

Public   Sub
Connect_To_Access_Database_using_OLEDB_And_DataTable(ByVal   cnstr   as
String, ByVal strQuery As String)

```
    Dim cn As System.Data.OleDb.OleDbConnection   = new
    System.Data.OleDb.OleDbConnection(cnstr)
    cn.Open()

    Dim da As System.Data.OleDb.OleDbDataAdapter   = new
System.Data.OleDb.OleDbDataAdapter(strQuery, cn)
    Dim dt as new System.Data.DataTable
    da.Fill(dt)
```

End Sub

OLEDB Connection and DataAdapter Using a DataView

Public Sub Connect_To_Access_Database_using_OLEDB_And_DataView(ByVal
cnstr as String, ByVal strQuery As String)

```
    Dim cn As System.Data.OleDb.OleDbConnection   = new
    System.Data.OleDb.OleDbConnection(cnstr)
    cn.Open()

    Dim da As System.Data.OleDb.OleDbDataAdapter   = new
System.Data.OleDb.OleDbDataAdapter(strQuery, cn)
    Dim dt as new System.Data.DataTable
    da.Fill(dt)
```

Dim dv as System.Data.DataView = dt.DefaultView

End Sub

OLEDB Command and DataAdapter Using a Dataset

Public Sub Connect_To_Access_Database_using_OLEDB_And_DataSet(ByVal cnstr as String, ByVal strQuery As String)

```
Dim cmd As System.Data.OleDb.OleDbCommand  = new
System.Data.OleDb.OleDbCommand()
cmd.Connection = new System.Data.OleDb.OleDbConnection
cmd.Connection.ConnectionString = cnstr
cmd.Connection.Open()

cmd.CommandType = 1
cmd.CommandText = strQuery
cmd.ExecuteNonquery()

Dim da As System.Data.OleDb.OleDbDataAdapter  = new
System.Data.OleDb.OleDbDataAdapter(cmd)
Dim ds as new System.Data.DataSet
da.Fill(ds)
```

End Sub

OLEDB Command and DataAdapter Using a DataTable

Public Sub Connect_To_Access_Database_using_OLEDB_And_DataTable(ByVal cnstr as String, ByVal strQuery As String)

```
Dim cmd As System.Data.OleDb.OleDbCommand  = new
System.Data.OleDb.OleDbCommand()
cmd.Connection = new System.Data.OleDb.OleDbConnection
cmd.Connection.ConnectionString = cnstr
cmd.Connection.Open()

cmd.CommandType = 1
cmd.CommandText = strQuery
cmd.ExecuteNonquery()

Dim da As System.Data.OleDb.OleDbDataAdapter  = new
System.Data.OleDb.OleDbDataAdapter(cmd)
Dim dt as new System.Data.DataTable
da.Fill(dt)


End Sub
```

OLEDB Command and DataAdapter Using a DataView

```
Public Sub Connect_To_Access_Database_using_OLEDB_And_DataView(ByVal
cnstr as String, ByVal strQuery As String)

    Dim cmd As System.Data.OleDb.OleDbCommand  = new
    System.Data.OleDb.OleDbCommand()
    cmd.Connection = new System.Data.OleDb.OleDbConnection
    cmd.Connection.ConnectionString = cnstr
    cmd.Connection.Open()

    cmd.CommandType = 1
    cmd.CommandText = strQuery
    cmd.ExecuteNonquery()

    Dim da As System.Data.OleDb.OleDbDataAdapter  = new
    System.Data.OleDb.OleDbDataAdapter(cmd)
    Dim dt as new System.Data.DataTable
    da.Fill(dt)
    Dim dv as System.Data.DataView = dt.DefaultView

End Sub
```

OLEDB DataAdapter Using a Dataset

Public Sub Connect_To_Access_Database_using_OLEDB_And_DataSet(ByVal cnstr as String, ByVal strQuery As String)

```
Dim da As System.Data.OleDb.OleDbDataAdapter  = new
System.Data.OleDb.OleDbDataAdapter(strQuery, cnstr)
Dim ds as new System.Data.DataSet
da.Fill(ds)
```

End Sub

OLEDB DataAdapter Using a DataTable

Public   Sub
Connect_To_Access_Database_using_OLEDB_And_DataTable(ByVal   cnstr   as
String, ByVal strQuery As String)

```
Dim da As System.Data.OleDb.OleDbDataAdapter  = new
System.Data.OleDb.OleDbDataAdapter(strQuery, cnstr)
Dim dt as new System.Data.DataTable
da.Fill(dt)
```

End Sub

OLEDB DataAdapter Using a DataView

Public Sub Connect_To_Access_Database_using_OLEDB_And_DataView(ByVal cnstr as String, ByVal strQuery As String)

```
Dim da As System.Data.OleDb.OleDbDataAdapter  = new
System.Data.OleDb.OleDbDataAdapter(strQuery, cnstr)
Dim dt as new System.Data.DataTable
da.Fill(dt)
Dim dv as System.Data.DataView = dt.DefaultView
```

End Sub

And there you have it! A book on all the various ways you can connect, manipulate and control how you work with an Access Database using VB.Net.

In the next book, we're going to start from where we left off here and cover ISAMS.

See you soon!

www.ingramcontent.com/pod-product-compliance
Lightning Source LLC
Chambersburg PA
CBHW070846070326
40690CB00009B/1724